C000225408

A Taste of the West Country

A collection of original recipes created by
Taste of the West award-winning chefs and producers

wemakemagazines

A catalogue record for this book is available
from the British Library.

ISBN 978-0-9933352-6-6

No part of this book shall be reproduced or
transmitted in any form or by any means, electronic
or mechanical, including photocopying, recording, or
by any information retrieval system without written
permission of the publisher.

Published by We Make Magazines Ltd
wemakemagazines.co.uk

Copyright © We Make Magazines Ltd
Photography © Guy Harrop Photos Ltd
Additional photography © We Make Magazines Ltd
Additional photography © David Griffen Photography

Editor: Jennie Cooper
Sub-editor: Raphael Chapell
Designer: Jeff Cooper

Thanks to Jo Hall, Julie Hutchins and Jody Spencer.

Although every precaution has been taken in the
preparation of this book, the publisher and authors
assume no responsibility for errors or omissions.
Neither is any liability assumed for damages resulting
from the use of this information contained herein.

wemakemagazines

Meat

Beef

Fillet steak with stir-fried vegetables and a black pepper sauce 40

Black garlic marinated beef fillet, wild garlic and pommes paillasson 42

Korean BBQ burger, kimchi, Gochujang ketchup, sesame mayonnaise, spring onion and shiso 52

Reuben rye bagels 64

Wasabi-seared beef tataki with watercress and cucumber ponzu salad 82

Chicken

Chicken Tom Kha (Thai chicken coconut soup) 70

Chicken nasi goreng with satay sauce and atjar tjampoer 72

Lamb

Rack of lamb in herb crust with roasted new potatoes, minted pea purée and lamb juice 46

Oven-roasted 3-bone rack of lamb, fondant potato, tenderstem broccoli, minted pea purée and rich wine jus 48

Pork

Faggots with onion gravy 54

Sausage-stuffed morel mushrooms, duxelle, nettle and wild garlic soup 58

Parmesan polenta, sausage ragù and basil 60

Cider vinegar roasted pork belly on an Asian apple cabbage salad with tamarind sauce 96

Sheep's cheese and Serrano ham croquettes with sun-blush tomato sauce 110

Pork tenderloin with sweet cider sauce, pomme purée, baby carrots, sautéed spinach, braised apple rings and cream cider jus 120

Venison

Ale-marinated venison medallions with champ mash, buttered kale, braised baby carrots and rich ale jus 116

Fish

Vegetarian

Sides

WESTWARD HO!
SLIPWAY & PEBBLE RIDGE
This Way

Desserts

Drinks

FOREWORD

Like many other businesses, food and drink producers have been facing unprecedented times. In these challenging circumstances, we feel it's important to support and celebrate the West Country's food and drink scene by bringing you this latest edition of *A Taste of the West Country* recipe book.

Now, more than ever, reduced food miles, product traceability and welfare standards are key topics for those working in the food industry and for consumers. Many of the producers who feature in this book offer field-to-fork schemes, while the restaurants source their food and drink from neighbouring towns, villages, or even their own kitchen gardens.

Every year, there are hundreds of entries into the coveted Taste of the West Awards. This latest edition of *A Taste of the West Country* is a pairing of the award-winning chefs and producers from Cornwall, Devon, Somerset and Dorset to bring you special recipes, using the finest local ingredients.

The dishes are created exclusively for this book, straight from the chef's kitchen. With produce readily available around the region, our clear layout and simple steps make it easy to create restaurant-style dishes at home for your friends and family.

By following these recipes, you can both impress your guests and support our food and drink industry; something I think we all feel is particularly important right now.

John Sheaves
Chief Executive, Taste of the West

All recipes serve 4, unless otherwise stated

Our West Country

Meet the people behind the food

The recipes in this book are designed to be prepared at home, but we encourage you to visit the award-winning pubs, restaurants and hotels featured to enjoy similar dishes prepared by the pros.

The producers' locations are also indicated with a page number where you can read their full story. Many of the producers in this book sell online – you can find website addresses on page 152.

The Victory Inn

"With a strong focus on sourcing local ingredients, its simple Local Supplier menu was a joy to see: a blackboard above the fireplace listed all the Cornish cheese on offer..."

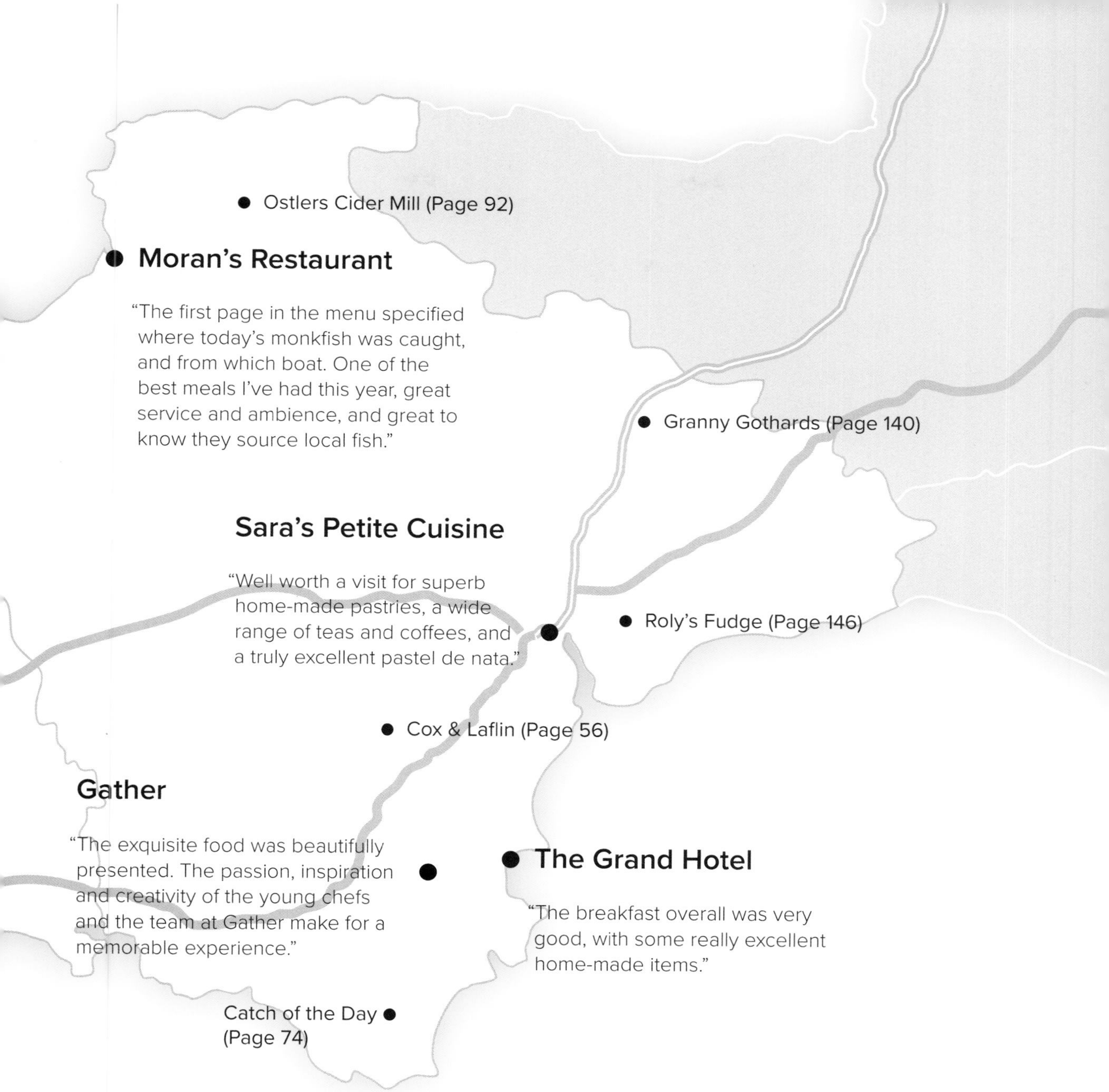

Ostlers Cider Mill (Page 92)

Moran's Restaurant

"The first page in the menu specified where today's monkfish was caught, and from which boat. One of the best meals I've had this year, great service and ambience, and great to know they source local fish."

Granny Gothards (Page 140)

Sara's Petite Cuisine

"Well worth a visit for superb home-made pastries, a wide range of teas and coffees, and a truly excellent pastel de nata."

Roly's Fudge (Page 146)

Cox & Laflin (Page 56)

Gather

"The exquisite food was beautifully presented. The passion, inspiration and creativity of the young chefs and the team at Gather make for a memorable experience."

The Grand Hotel

"The breakfast overall was very good, with some really excellent home-made items."

Catch of the Day (Page 74)

Jean Edwards, Partner, Deli Farm Charcuterie

Rebekah Paterson, Owner, Ostlers Cider Mill

Head Chef Alex Skelton (left) and Owner/Chef Matt Henderson (right), The Victory Inn

Harrison Brockington, Chef and Owner, Gather

Andrew Cox, Owner, Cox & Laflin

Frankie Moran, Head Chef/Proprietor, Moran's Restaurant

Sara Felix, Owner, Sara's Petite Cuisine

Luis Sargeant, Sous Chef, and Owen Isaacs, Head Chef, The Grand Hotel

PHOTO: DAVID GRIFFEN

Thatchers Cider (Page 118)

Fussels Fine Foods (Page 86)

SOMERSET

Beeden & Beeden
(Page 130)

P&K Meats
(Pages 38 and 44)

The Eastbury Hotel & Spa, Seasons Restaurant

The Blackmore Vale Butchery (Page 50)

The Lordleaze Hotel

"The meal presentation was first-class, and the quality of the food was excellent. My steak was delicious and cooked perfectly as ordered. There was just the right quantity on the plate."

DORSET

The Book & Bucket Cheese Company (Page 106)

Palmers Brewery (Page 112)

Fordington Gin (Page 124)

The Three Horseshoes

The Watercress Company (Page 103)

The Wasabi Company (Page 81)

The Eastbury Hotel & Spa, Seasons Restaurant

"This was, without doubt, the best meal that I have eaten at a restaurant in Dorset in 25 years. It was very good - dishes were well thought through, well balanced, and flavours were excellent."

The Three Horseshoes

"The Three Horseshoes is a thriving local pub as well as being a worthy destination for high-quality eating out."

Charlie and Zara Beeden, Owners, Beeden & Beeden

Matthew Street, Executive Chef, The Eastbury Hotel & Spa, Seasons Restaurant

Tom Owen, Owner, and Joe Nagy, Head Chef, The Lordleaze Hotel

Darren Batten, Head Brewer, Palmers Brewery

Eleanor Thatcher, fifth-generation cider maker, Thatchers

Jaap and Hannah Schep, Owners, The Three Horseshoes

Ros Nelmes, Master Creator, Fordington Gin

Peter Morgan, Owner, Book & Bucket Cheese Company

Andy Fussell and Lizzy Etheridge, Fussels Fine Foods

David Turton, Wasabi Production Manager, The Wasabi Company

Luke Beech, Watercress Production Manager,
The Watercress Company

Paul Jeffery, Owner, P&K Meats

BEEF

What makes an award-winning butcher's shop? Sourcing and striving for perfection, says Paul Jeffery, Proprietor of P&K Meats in Street, Somerset

Paul, alongside his partner Kayleigh, owns and runs this award-winning business – supplying to the public, as well as pubs, restaurants, hotels and schools, and many other establishments across Somerset, Bristol and Avon, Dorset and Devon.

Paul enjoys experimenting with the butchery process to gain more understanding and knowledge of the optimum ageing time for various cuts of meat – in particular, his T-bone, sirloin and ribeye steaks. "To date, the longest we have cured our beef products for is 65 days, which produced amazing results with an incredible depth of flavour."

This business takes great pride in the products it sources and where they come from, and pays great attention to detail when producing them. "One particular area I am personally very proud of is our salt chamber, where we dry-age various products to enhance their flavour. We use Himalayan salt bricks to create the perfect pH balance to dry and age the products to our desired specification," he explains.

"Butchery is my passion and a big part of who I am – the love I have for what I do keeps me motivated and striving for perfection," Paul concludes.

Award-winning products
2019 – 3-Bone Rack of Lamb: Silver; Fillet Steak (8oz): Silver
2020 – Pork & Apple Burger: Gold; Dry-Aged Farm Wilder T-Bone Steak (8oz): Gold; Dry-Aged Farm Wilder Sirloin Steak (10oz): Gold; Pork, Honey & Mustard Sausages: Silver; Pork & Apple Sausages: Silver; Pork Sausages: Silver

"Butchery is my passion and a big part of who I am – the love I have for what I do keeps me motivated and striving for perfection."

Fillet steak with stir-fried vegetables and a black pepper sauce

Recipe by Francesca Moran, Head Chef/Proprietor, Moran's Restaurant & Bar, Westward Ho!, Devon

Ingredients

4 P&K Meats' Fillet Steaks
70g celery, sliced
3 cloves of garlic, crushed
10g black peppercorns, crushed
200g mushrooms, sliced
100g green beans, chopped
1 red pepper, sliced
1 white onion, sliced
2 tbsp of Fussels Fine Foods' Extra Virgin Rapeseed Oil
3 tbsp oyster sauce
6 tbsp soy sauce
1 beef stock cube
200ml water
3 tsp sugar
½ tsp salt
Bunch of coriander
Black sesame seeds (optional)
Sliced spring onions (optional for garnish)

To prepare the fillet steaks

1. Generously cover the steaks with rock salt and pepper, then cover in rapeseed oil.
2. Add the soy sauce, one teaspoon of sugar and massage into the meat.
3. Cover and leave in the fridge to marinate for as long as possible (overnight is best).

To make the black pepper paste

1. Place the celery, garlic, peppercorns and the coriander stalks into a food processor and blend until smooth.
2. Once the steak has returned to room temperature, pan-fry until medium rare for two to five minutes each side, depending on thickness (or however desired). Leave on a board to rest.
3. Heat two tablespoons of rapeseed oil in a hot wok, then add the mushrooms, red pepper, onion and green beans, and stir regularly.
4. Add the oyster sauce, three tablespoons of soy sauce, stock cube, two teaspoons of sugar, salt and the water to the wok. Continue to cook for a further five minutes, then add the pepper paste to taste (recommend three or four teaspoons).
5. Using a ladle with holes, place the vegetables onto a plate with just a little of the sauce, then thinly slice the steak and fan over the vegetables.
6. Pour the sauce from the wok into dip pots to serve with the steak, then garnish the dish with coriander, black sesame seeds and spring onions.

Chef's tip: This meal goes perfectly with rice, but also pairs beautifully with chips or new potatoes.

Black garlic marinated beef fillet, wild garlic and pommes paillasson

Recipe by Harrison Brockington, Head Chef, Gather, Totnes, Devon

Ingredients

For the beef
2 P&K Meats' 8oz Fillet Steak
Beef sauce (optional for serving)

For the black garlic marinade
50g wild garlic
18g black garlic
60g water
Salt and pepper

For the pommes paillasson
300g starchy potatoes (such as Maris Piper)
250g beef dripping, melted
7g thyme, chopped
7g salt

For finishing the dish
15g butter
4 sprigs of thyme
2 cloves of garlic, crushed
A couple of handfuls of wild garlic leaves

Chef's tip: Serve with your preferred steak sauce. I used a beef and red wine jus but it would go just as well with peppercorn or Béarnaise sauce.

Method

Add a difference to your steak and chips using the rich umami flavours of the black garlic to create a caramelised crust on your steak. Pomme Paillasson is a shredded potato pancake, crisp on the outside and soft inside (similar to a hash brown).

To make the marinade

1. In a hot oven, bake the wild garlic until dark and crispy, then remove from the oven.
2. Blend the black garlic and the cooked wild garlic with water to create a paste, and then season.
3. Once the garlic marinade is cool, pour it over the beef and refrigerate for a few hours or overnight.

To make the pommes paillasson

1. Peel and grate the potatoes, then place in a saucepan and cover with the beef dripping.
2. Cook over a low heat until the potatoes are done (look for a gluey consistency).
3. Pour the potatoes into a sieve, draining any excess fat, then mix in the thyme and salt.
4. Pour the potato mixture into a tray lined with clingfilm – aim for it to be around 2cm thick.
5. Place a weight on top of the mixture (a plate or tray), refrigerate for a few hours until completely cooled, or overnight.
6. Once chilled, notice how the starch has set the potatoes into a solid block. Portion this into neat rectangles, then deep-fry in oil at 180°C until golden brown and crispy (this can be done in either a deep fryer or frying pan).

To cook the beef

1. In a hot pan, fry the steak to your preference, basting in the butter, garlic and thyme. Remove from the pan, then rest.
2. In the same pan, sauté some wild garlic leaves.

To serve

Dress the plate by arranging the sautéed wild garlic, alongside a portion of the potatoes, and carve the fillet into slices to plate (half a fillet per portion).

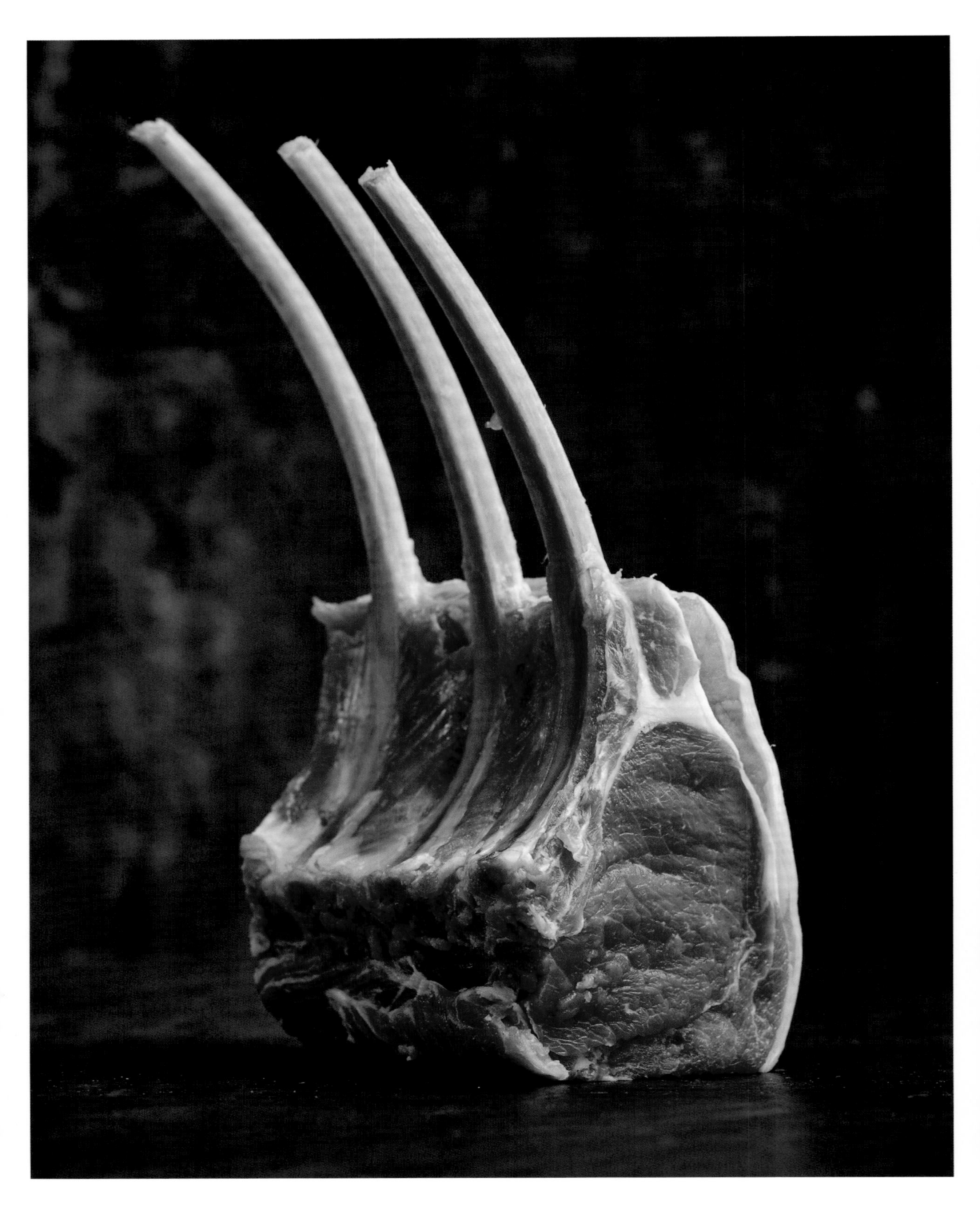

LAMB

Sourcing is key to P&K Meats' success, says Paul Jeffery, proprietor of this award-winning butchers in Street, Somerset

Paul, and partner Kayleigh, own and run P&K Meats, supplying their award-winning meat to the public, as well as to hotels, pubs, restaurants and schools, and other businesses across Somerset, Bristol and Avon, Dorset and Devon.

Paul sources the majority of his products from farms in the south-west, and tries to use the closest abattoirs to reduce food miles and carbon footprint. As well as supplying products like lamb, beef, pork, poultry and game, P&K Meats produces its own sausages, burgers and faggots. "We also have a section in the shop where we sell local dairy products and our popular cooked hams, along with a selection of Italian and Spanish products such as pancetta, chorizos and prosciutto," Paul adds.

Paul's work is more than a day job. "I have a passion for local, well-produced products within my personal life too, and consider myself a foodie at heart. I love trying new taste and flavour combinations, and enjoy eating in a variety of food establishments – from local restaurants on our doorstep to highly-renowned Michelin-starred restaurants up and down the country," he concludes.

Award-winning products
2019 – 3-Bone Rack of Lamb: Silver; Fillet Steak (8oz): Silver
2020 – Pork & Apple Burger: Gold; Dry-Aged Farm Wilder T-Bone Steak (8oz): Gold; Dry-Aged Farm Wilder Sirloin Steak (10oz): Gold; Pork, Honey & Mustard Sausages: Silver; Pork & Apple Sausages: Silver; Pork Sausages: Silver

"I have a passion for local, well-produced products within my personal life too, and consider myself a foodie at heart."

Rack of lamb in herb crust with roasted new potatœs, minted pea purée and lamb juice

Recipe by Jœ Nagy, Head Chef, Lordleaze Hotel, Chard, Somerset

Ingredients
4 P&K Meats' 3-Bone Rack of Lamb
2 tsp rosemary, chopped
1 tsp thyme, chopped
2 cloves of garlic, minced
Salt and pepper
2 tbsp extra virgin olive oil
Few cubes of butter
New potatoes (4 per person)

For the pea purée
200g frozen peas
Salt
Lemon juice
Fresh mint leaves

For the herb crust
½ cup breadcrumbs
4 tbsp Dijon mustard
1 clove of garlic
Olive oil
Salt
Freshly ground black pepper
A few leaves each of rosemary, spinach and basil

For the sauce
1 clove of garlic
Lamb stock
25g butter, unsalted
Salt and pepper

To marinate the lamb
Rub the racks all over with a mixture of rosemary, thyme and garlic, then leave to marinate in the fridge overnight.

To make the pea purée
1. Bring a large pan of salted water to the boil and blanch the peas for three minutes.
2. Add to a blender – with a little water and mint – for two to three minutes, adding more liquid in small amounts. Aim for a fairly thick, smooth purée consistency.
3. Season with salt and a squeeze of fresh lemon juice.

To cook the lamb
1. Remove the lamb from the fridge around two hours before cooking and preheat the oven to 220°C.
2. Score the fat, sprinkle with salt and pepper, wrap bones in foil and place in a pan, fat-side up.
3. Roast at a high heat until the meat begins to brown, reducing the temperature to finish off cooking for about 10 minutes, or until the surface of the roast is browned.
4. Meanwhile, boil the new potatoes until soft, place them on a baking tray, season with rosemary, salt and pepper.
5. Drizzle with olive oil and a couple of butter cubes, and roast at 180°C for 20–25 minutes.

To make the herb crust
1. Place the leaves in a food processor along with the garlic, a large pinch of salt, freshly ground black pepper and the breadcrumbs.
2. Add in just enough olive oil to make the mixture moist.
3. Spread the mustard onto the rack of lamb, then coat the thick, meaty side with the breadcrumb mixture.
4. Lower the oven temperature to 150°C. Cook the lamb for another 10 minutes, or until a meat thermometer inserted into the thickest part of the meat reads between 55–58°C for medium rare.
5. Remove from the oven and rest for five to 10 minutes before serving.

To make the sauce and serve
1. Add the garlic and rosemary to a pan with the meat juices, then add butter.
2. Simmer for three to five minutes and serve on top of the dish.

Roasted 3-bone lamb rack, fondant potato, tenderstem broccoli, pea purée and wine jus

Recipe by Owen Isaacs, Executive Head Chef, The Grand Hotel, Torquay, Devon

Ingredients

8oz P&K Meats' 3-Bone Rack of Lamb x 4
½ bottle of red wine (Burgundy works well)
2 large banana shallots, finely chopped
200ml rich lamb stock reduction (pre-made for jus)
20g redcurrant jelly
2 sprigs of rosemary
3 cloves of garlic, finely chopped
80g butter, unsalted
Vegetable oil
Salt and pepper
Fondant potato, pre-cooked (enough for four)
Tenderstem broccoli, pre-cooked (enough for four)
Minted pea purée, pre-cooked (enough for four)
Watercress sprigs (to garnish)

To prepare the meat

French-trim the lamb rack (or ask the butcher to do this for you), score the fat and set aside ready for cooking.

To cook the dish

1. Preheat the oven to 180°C/160°C fan/gas mark 4.
2. Pan-fry the shallots over a medium heat for a few minutes, or until golden.
3. Add the lamb stock and red wine, and simmer to reduce for around 20 minutes.
4. Add the redcurrant jelly and simmer to reduce for another five minutes.
5. Cut the fondant potatoes and place them in a tray with the lamb stock reduction, seasoning, two garlic cloves and a sprig of rosemary. The stock should not cover the vegetables.
6. Place a knob of butter on the potato tops and roast in the oven for around 10–15 minutes, or until golden brown.
7. Pan-sear the lamb rack, fat-side down for two minutes, along with the remaining rosemary sprig and garlic clove. Add some seasoning, then turn over and sear on the other side for another minute.
8. Once seared, turn the meat fat-side down again and roast in the oven for 14 minutes.
9. Remove from the oven and set aside to rest.
10. Cook the tenderstem broccoli to your liking and once done, sauté in a knob of the butter.
11. Arrange the vegetables on a warmed plate, slice the lamb rack and place on top of the potato.
12. Add 55g of butter to the stock in the pan and simmer to thicken. Once it has turned glossy, carefully pour some around the lamb.
13. Garnish with the watercress and minted pea purée.

BURGERS & FAGGOTS

Gavin Keen, General Manager of The Blackmore Vale Butchery, near Henstridge in Somerset, enjoys product development and perfecting recipes to create his award-winning products

Specialising in local, dry-aged beef, grass-fed lamb and free-range pork from Somerset, Dorset and Wiltshire, Gavin and his team make several different flavours of sausages and burgers using its own recipes. These include gluten-free varieties, along with a range of award-winning faggots and pork pies. The Blackmore Vale Butchery's products are found in many local farm shops, as well as being served in local restaurants.

"Our faggots have been popular since we first opened in 2006. Our recipe is actually a mixture of two recipes which were passed down to me that I have tweaked, based on customer feedback. Once we found the sweet spot, we never looked back. We only use local meat, specific cuts and seasonings to get the required taste and texture needed," Gavin explains. "Our prime beef burgers are made using specifically chosen cuts, lightly seasoned and hand-pressed into either 4oz, 6oz or 8oz patties. They are definitely one of our bestsellers in BBQ season."

"I really enjoy product development and creating something that customers are wowed by, such as lamb bacon, black garlic flat-iron steaks or stuffed meat bombs. I get a lot of satisfaction from working with local smallholders and farmers, seeing how they grow their own meat sales with the help of our butchery department and services we offer."

"Starting the business from scratch and working tremendously hard to build up our reputation was really tough, as was relocating into a purpose-built butchery at the start of the first lockdown and working through Covid restrictions. But we coped well," Gavin adds.

Award-winning products
2019 – Homemade Faggots: Gold; Prime Handmade Beef Burger: Silver

Korean BBQ burger, kimchi, Gochujang ketchup, sesame mayonnaise, spring onion and shiso

Recipe by Matthew Street, Executive Chef, The Eastbury Hotel & Spa, Seasons Restaurant, Sherborne, Dorset

Ingredients

For the burgers
4 brioche or hokkaido buns
8 The Blackmore Vale Butchery's Prime Handmade Beef Burgers
200g kimchi
16 shiso leaves
8 cheese slices

For the marinade
100ml soy sauce
100g brown sugar
4 cloves of garlic, crushed
1-inch piece of fresh ginger, grated
1 tbsp sesame oil
50ml apple or pear juice
1 spring onion, finely sliced

For the ketchup
1 tbsp ketchup
2 tbsp gochujang chilli paste
2 tsp light soy sauce
½ tbsp honey or maple syrup

For the mayonnaise
1 tsp sesame oil
1 tsp garlic, minced
1 tsp sesame seeds, toasted

For serving
Handful of spring onions, finely chopped

To make the marinade, ketchup and mayonnaise, and prepare the burgers

1. Combine the marinade ingredients and then cover the burgers in the marinade for at least 20 minutes.
2. Press the meat so it's flat. It should be the same size in diameter as the bun and no thicker than 2cm high.
3. Warm a griddle plate or a BBQ.
4. Mix the mayonnaise ingredients first, then the ketchup mixture and put both in the fridge.

To cook the dish

1. Once the griddle or BBQ is hot, quickly toast the halved burger buns on the heat.
2. Cook the marinated burgers on each side for around one minute.
3. After they have coloured on both sides, add the cheese slices, followed by the kimchi. Cover the burgers with a lid or a deep tray to steam cook for a further minute (or close the lid on the BBQ).
4. While the burgers are finishing off, take the base of a bun, top with the ketchup and two shiso leaves.
5. Spread the sesame mayonnaise and the spring onions on the top half of the bun, slide the burgers onto the bottom half, then close up the burger.

Faggots with onion gravy

Ingredients

4 The Blackmore Vale Butchery's Handmade Faggots

For the gravy

1 tbsp oil
1 tbsp butter
2 onions, finely sliced
2 tsp brown sugar
1 clove of garlic, crushed
2 sprigs of fresh thyme
1 tbsp plain flour
1 glass red wine
400ml beef stock
Salt and pepper

Method

1. Over a medium heat, fry the faggots in a little oil on all sides. Remove from the frying pan once browned.
2. Using the same pan to soak up the flavours of the faggots, melt the butter and add the onions and sugar. Stir regularly until golden and lightly caramelised.
3. Add the garlic and thyme, and then cook for a further five minutes.
4. Stir the flour in well, then add the red wine and let it bubble until it has reduced by about half.
5. Gradually add the stock and stir continuously until the gravy has thickened.
6. Place the faggots in a shallow casserole dish and pour over the gravy. Cover with a lid or foil and bake for one hour at 180°C/160°C fan/gas mark 4 until cooked through.

SAUSAGES

Field-to-plate farming is of utmost importance for Andrew Cox, owner at Cox & Laflin Butchers, Ullacombe Farm, Dartmoor, Devon

This award-winning butchers has its shop located just below Haytor on Dartmoor. It prides itself on providing the best locally sourced produce. From inception, Cox & Laflin's aim has been to give customers a fully transparent service, a true field-to-plate process from carefully nurtured, grass-fed stock to neat, efficient and well-presented final cuts of meat.

Andrew explains: "We only supply a few establishments local to us on Dartmoor. Our main aim is to supply our customers with top quality produce from the area. We know where all our meat comes from."

What does it take to make an award-winning sausage? "When it comes to making our pork sausages, it took a while to get it right, with a lot of going back to the chalkboard. But, we cracked it!" After much discussion and tasting, Andrew says: "It was all about the pork. We have a great relationship with our pig farmer and after a few conversations, we went with a cross between a Tamworth pig and a Duroc pig. It produces, in our opinion, the best pork and makes amazing tasting sausages," he enthuses.

"Once we got the pork right, we played around with some different herbs and seasonings, and came up with our very popular Plain Pork Sausages," adds Andrew.

Award-winning products
2019 – Chicken Sausages: Gold; Plain Pork Sausages: Silver

"Our main aim is to supply our customers with top quality produce from the area."

Sausage-stuffed morel mushrooms, duxelle, nettle and wild garlic soup

Recipe by Harrison Brockington, Head Chef, Gather, Totnes, Devon

Ingredients

2 Cox & Laflin Butchers' Plain Pork Sausages
8 morel mushrooms, washed

For the mushroom duxelle

2 banana shallots
2 cloves of garlic
250g morel mushrooms, washed and finely chopped
15ml Madeira
25g butter
50ml chicken/pork stock
4 wild garlic flowers

For the wild garlic and nettle soup

100g nettles
100g wild garlic
1 banana shallot
1 clove of garlic
200ml double cream
50ml chicken/pork stock
25g butter

To prepare the sausages

1. Remove the sausage meat from the skins, season, then place in a piping bag.
2. Pipe eight whole morel mushrooms with the sausage stuffing and refrigerate.
3. Finely dice the shallots and garlic, and split between two saucepans.

To make the duxelle

1. In one of the pans, sweat the shallots and garlic on a low heat. Do not let them colour.
2. Add the chopped mushrooms, and when softened, add a splash of Madeira.
3. Reduce until thickened, then keep warm.

To cook the stuffed mushrooms

1. Add 25g of butter to a pan and gently fry the stuffed mushrooms.
2. Once the butter is browned, add the stock. Shake the pan, so the butter and stock emulsify into a glaze, then coat the mushrooms in the glaze.
3. Double-check the filling is cooked by using a temperature probe (which should read 74°C), then set it aside for plating.

To make the soup

1. In the other saucepan, sweat the shallots and garlic on a low heat. Do not let them colour.
2. Add the wild garlic and nettles, and once wilted, add the double cream and the stock.
3. Bring to the boil for three minutes, then blend in the butter (using a stick blender) and pass through a fine sieve.
4. Keep warm and reserve.

To serve

1. Place the mushroom duxelle in four warmed bowls, and top with the sausage-stuffed mushrooms.
2. Blitz the soup, and spoon it over the dish, covering the duxelle but keeping the mushroom tops uncoated.
3. Garnish with a few wild garlic flowers.

Parmesan polenta, sausage ragù and basil

Recipe by Matthew Street, Executive Chef, The Eastbury Hotel & Spa, Seasons Restaurant, Sherborne, Dorset

Ingredients

For the sausage ragù

8 Cox & Laflin Butchers' Plain Pork Sausages
3 tbsp olive oil
6 cloves of garlic, minced
400g tin tomatoes
1 large onion, chopped
1 tbsp tomato paste
100ml dry red wine (optional)
1 tsp sugar
1 tsp dried/fresh oregano
2 tsp salt
Pinch of chilli flakes
8 basil leaves, roughly chopped
Black pepper to taste
1 tbsp balsamic vinegar

For the polenta

1.8l of stock, or water
2 tbsp olive oil
350g dry polenta
450ml double cream
200g Parmesan, grated
3 tsp salt
½ tsp black pepper

For serving

Grated Parmesan
Basil pesto
Olive oil
Basil leaves

Method

1. Preheat the oven to 170°C/ 155°C fan/gas mark 3.
2. Take four sausages, remove the skin and break up into small pieces.
3. Cook the other four sausages in the oven for 12 minutes.

To make the ragù

1. Warm the olive oil, add the onions, garlic and sausage meat pieces until lightly browned, then add the red wine and reduce by half.
2. Add all the other ragù ingredients and simmer on a low heat for 15 minutes. Add the whole cooked sausages to the ragù when they've finished cooking in the oven.

To make the polenta

1. While the ragù is cooking, heat the stock or water in a large saucepan. When hot, gradually add the polenta.
2. Slowly mix with a whisk and finish adding the polenta before all the other ingredients.

To serve

1. Check the polenta for seasoning, then plate it up between four warmed bowls.
2. Top with the ragù, ensuring each plate gets a sausage.
3. Finish this with a drizzle of basil pesto, a sprinkling of grated Parmesan, olive oil and a couple of basil leaves.

CHARCUTERIE

Jean Edwards, Partner at Deli Farm Charcuterie in Delabole, Cornwall, talks all things curing and what it takes to create award-winning products

Supplying products nationwide, Jean puts her company's success down to ingredients and careful curing: "We use local meats in all our products, with 90% of our pork coming from a family-run farm about 12 miles from us. Low food miles and lots of provenance – the balance comes from the West Country."

"For the salami, the meat is mixed with salts, cures, freshly ground herbs and spices, and is then fermented for the first 18 hours to start the process. The salamis are then hung up to slowly dry and mature. The whole process takes about two months," explains Jean.

She continues: "For our cured meats, a dry rub of salts, cure, cane sugar and spices are rubbed in, which takes a month, then they are hung up to dry and mature. This process can take anywhere from two months to two years, depending on the size of the joint you are curing. Weight checks and various tests are done at the end of the process to validate that it is a stable, ambient product.

A pinch of imagination, together with what's exciting customers' appetites, fuels Jean and her team with ideas for new recipes. "We carry out small, trial batches to see whether the recipe works, or if it needs tweaking. We also listen to customers and see what's trending." Jean adds that creating new products is a highlight for her, as is quality control: "Periodic tasting has to be done to ensure continuity!"

In terms of accolades, Deli Farm Charcuterie has its fair share. "Our most exciting moment was being selected as one of the final three for the BBC Food and Farming Awards, and our proudest moment was winning Supreme Champion at the Taste of the West Awards," Jean concludes.

Award-winning products
2019 – Apple Smoked Cooked Ham: Silver; Cornish Real Corned Beef, Cornish Pastrami: Commended; Cornishman's Relish: Gold
2020 – Black Olive Salami, Fennel & Anise Salami, Honey & Mustard Glazed Smoked Ham, Duck Prosciutto: Gold; Cornish Pastrami: Commended

Reuben rye bagels

Recipe by Matthew Street, Executive Chef,
The Eastbury Hotel & Spa, Seasons Restaurant, Sherborne, Dorset

Ingredients

For the bagels
350ml oat milk
60g butter
½ cube of fresh yeast, or 7g dry yeast
1 tbsp maple syrup
400g rye flour
200g white flour
Handful of porridge oats
2–3 tsp salt
1 egg white

For the water bath
1l water
100g baking soda
1 tbsp salt

For the Russian dressing
1 tbsp onion, finely chopped
300g mayonnaise
200g ketchup-style chilli sauce
4 tsp horseradish sauce
1 tsp Tabasco sauce
1 tsp Worcestershire sauce
¼ tsp sweet paprika
Pinch of fine sea salt

For the bagel filling
800g Deli Farm Charcuterie's Cornish Pastrami
8 Swiss cheese slices
400g sauerkraut

To make the bagels

1. Warm the milk, butter, yeast and maple syrup until everything has dissolved.
2. Add the flour and salt to the mixture, then knead into a dough.
3. Cover and allow to rise for one to two hours in a warm place.
4. Put the dough on a well-floured work surface and knead again.
5. Split into eight and form balls. Flatten them a little, and then take the back of a wooden spoon to form the hole in the middle.
6. Let the bagels rise again for about 20 minutes.
7. Preheat the oven to 180°C/165°C fan/gas mark 4.
8. In a pan, bring the water, mixed with the baking soda and salt to a boil, then remove from the heat and add the bagels (two to three at a time).
9. Allow them to sit in the water bath for 30 seconds, making sure they are fully covered.
10. Remove, tap off any excess water and place on a baking tray.
11. Brush with the egg white and sprinkle with the salt and oats.
12. Bake for 20 minutes (*Chef's tip*: bake for 15 minutes, then turn and bake for another 5 minutes).
13. Use this time to combine all the ingredients for the Russian dressing.

To assemble the dish

1. Split the bagels in half, toast them under the grill, then spread the dressing on both sides.
2. On a tray, stack 100g pastrami per portion, top with a cheese slice and place under the grill to melt.
3. Next, add 50g of the sauerkraut per portion and put back under the grill to warm for a few seconds.
4. Take the pastrami, cheese and sauerkraut stack and sandwich this between the bagel.

Cornish scallops with fennel and anise salami, and kimchi

Recipe by Matt Henderson, Head Chef/Owner, The Victory Inn, St Mawes, Cornwall

Ingredients

4 large scallops
4 pieces of Deli Farm Charcuterie's Fennel & Anise Salami
Kimchi (Vadasz raw kimchi is great)
1 tsp unflavoured cooking oil
4 apple pieces, thinly sliced

Method

1. Place the salami on a tray and warm slightly under a grill.
2. Heat a pan and add the oil when hot.
3. Cook the scallops on a high heat for two minutes on one side and then a further minute on the other – they may need a little longer depending on their size, but be careful not to overcook.
4. Leave to rest for two minutes, while you plate up.

To serve

Place an apple slice on each plate and add the desired amount of kimchi onto the middle of the apple. Put a scallop on top, then add the salami on top again, and enjoy!

CHICKEN

Chicken Tom Kha (Thai chicken coconut soup)

Recipe by Francesca Moran, Head Chef/Proprietor, Moran's Restaurant & Bar, Westward Ho!, Devon

Ingredients
800ml coconut milk
800ml chicken stock
400g chicken, sliced
½ red onion, thinly sliced
4 tbsp fish sauce
4 tbsp lime juice
3 tbsp sugar (preferably palm sugar)
20g ginger, thinly sliced (preferably galangal)
12 kaffir lime leaves
2 lemongrass sticks, sliced
200g mushrooms
2 tomatoes, sliced
Bunch of coriander
Chilli oil (optional)
2 spring onions, thinly sliced

Method
1. Add the chicken stock, with the lime leaves and ginger, to a saucepan on a medium heat.
2. Smash the lemongrass to release its flavour, add to the stock and bring to the boil.
3. Once boiling, add the mushrooms, tomatoes, red onion, coconut milk and sliced chicken, then bring down to a simmer for three to four minutes.
4. Add the fish sauce, lime juice and sugar, then allow to cook for one more minute.
5. Serve into four bowls and garnish with coriander, chilli oil and spring onion.

Chef's tip: This makes a perfect starter, or serve with steamed rice for a light lunch.

Chicken nasi goreng with satay sauce and atjar tjampoer

Recipe by Jaap Schep, Head Chef, The Three Horseshoes, Burton Bradstock, Dorset

Ingredients
4 chicken breasts
600g basmati rice, cooked
100g carrots, diced
100g celery, diced
100g onion, diced
100g leeks, sliced
10g ground turmeric
20ml oil
4 cloves of garlic
30g fresh ginger
300g smooth peanut butter
300ml water
100g soft brown sugar
50ml light soy sauce
1 red chilli
1 bunch of fresh coriander
4 eggs
1 tub of crispy fried onions
1 bag of prawn crackers

Chef's tip: This recipe works equally well with pork fillet, or use halloumi for a meat-free alternative.

To cook the chicken nasi goreng

1. Blend the turmeric, oil, garlic and ginger to make the nasi goreng paste.
2. Cut the chicken into strips, skewer them and marinate in two tablespoons of the soy sauce.
3. Add the paste to a large frying pan on a medium heat. Cook for two minutes, then add the carrots, celery, onions and leeks, and cook for a further two minutes.
4. Add the cooked basmati rice and keep stirring for four minutes until hot.

For the satay sauce

1. In a saucepan, bring the peanut butter, water, brown sugar, the rest of the soy sauce and chopped chilli slowly to the boil, stirring constantly. Add more water if needed for a thick running consistency.
2. Grill or pan-fry the chicken skewers for four minutes on each side, until thoroughly cooked.
3. Fry the eggs in a pan.

To serve

Place the rice in the middle of a plate and serve with the chicken skewers and satay sauce. Put the fried egg on top, garnish with coriander and crispy fried onions. Serve some atjar tjampoer (see page 98) and prawn crackers on the side.

FISH

Rikki Down, Director of Catch of the Day and Salcombe Smokies in Kingsbridge, Devon, talks about how his team, passion and experience have led to him winning awards

Rikki explains: "We sell a huge variety of fresh, locally sourced fish and shellfish, as well as a selection of frozen products to complement our Salcombe Smokies and smoked salmon which are all smoked on our premises in Kingsbridge. I would like to tell you about the process but it's a closely guarded secret! I can tell you that we only use natural processes to enhance the flavours to bring out the best in the product – this has remained the same for over 60 years."

Catch of the Day supplies throughout the UK by mail order, but mostly people travel from Devon and Cornwall to collect their "smokies fix" as it is known locally. "We don't feel like this is a job. we love it and spend every day with big smiles, chatting to customers about daily life."

Rikki believes in teamwork. "The true stars of the shop, and driving force behind us at Catch of the Day, are Darren and Emma Carter, along with my eldest son, Ben, who was our Head Smoker at the time. They were the ones who encouraged me to enter into our first Taste of the West awards."

It hasn't been easy for the team, as Rikki explains: "A couple of years ago, after we got through to the second round in the Taste of the West awards, we had a serious fire in one of our kilns. We didn't know if the business would make it through without the smokies. At the same time, Ben was admitted to hospital with a spinal abscess which has left him paralysed for life. Before this, as Head Smoker, he spent months sampling new techniques and smoking times, and developed the smokies into the product you can buy today. They have always been the best you can get, but he took them to an award-winning level."

"We have a passion for the finest seafood and we make sure we are the best at what we do. With over 60 years together in the industry, we believe we have the knowledge and experience to make sure our customers can enjoy the best produce on the market."

Award-winning products
2019 – Salcombe Smokies: Gold; Smoked Salmon Pâté: Silver; Salcombe Smoked Salmon: Commended

Smoked salmon in a spicy Thai salad

Recipe by Francesca Moran, Head Chef/Proprietor, Moran's Restaurant & Bar, Westward Ho!, Devon

Ingredients

250g Salcombe Smoked Salmon from Catch of the Day
10 cherry tomatoes, sliced
¼ cucumber, thinly sliced
1 red onion, thinly sliced
3 tbsp fish sauce
3 tbsp lime juice
3 chillies, sliced (optional)
2 tsp sugar
1 tbsp sriracha chilli sauce
6 tbsp water
1 stock cube
150g peanuts, crushed
4 spring onions, sliced
Bunch of coriander

Method

1. Add the fish sauce, lime juice, sugar, sriracha, water and stock cube to a bowl and mix until the sugar and stock cube have dissolved.
2. Taste and add the chillies if desired.
3. Slice the salmon into spoon-sized pieces and add to the dressing mix, leaving to marinate for only a few minutes.
4. Add the tomatoes, cucumber, red onion, coriander leaves and half the crushed peanuts, then mix, ensuring all ingredients are covered with the dressing.
5. Serve onto a bowl or plate that has a lip around the edge to allow for a generous amount of sauce.
6. Top with the remaining crushed peanuts, and garnish with spring onion and coriander.

Chef's tip: Prepare the ingredients in advance, but only make the dish minutes before serving to ensure a light, fresh, crunchy salad.

Smoked mackerel pâté and sweet pickled dill cucumbers

Recipe by Matthew Street, Executive Chef,
The Eastbury Hotel & Spa, Seasons Restaurant, Sherborne, Dorset

Ingredients

For the pickled dill cucumbers
500g ridged pickling cucumbers
40g sea salt
1 tsp black pepper
1 tsp coriander seeds
1 tsp yellow mustard seeds
5 cloves of garlic
Pinch of mace
1 tbsp turmeric
2 bay leaves
1 onion
450g white pickling vinegar
80g sugar
Handful of dill (save a pinch for seasoning)

For the pâté
400g Catch of the Day's Salcombe Smokies (mackerel)
100g crème fraîche
40g horseradish
½ a lemon, juiced
1 tsp each of salt and pepper

To prepare the pickled cucumbers in advance

1. Slice the pickling cucumbers, cover with salt and leave overnight. Drain and wash the following morning.
2. Put all the dry spices in a saucepan and lightly toast them.
3. Add the onion, vinegar and sugar, and warm to dissolve the sugar. As it cools, add the dill.
4. Pack the washed cucumbers into jars, pour over the vinegar and leave for two weeks.

To make the mackerel pâté

1. Remove the skin and any bones from the smoked fillets, saving 100g of the mackerel for serving.
2. Blitz the rest of the mackerel in a food processor – along with the crème fraîche, horseradish, lemon juice and seasoning – until you have a smooth pâté and then place into four tins, or ramekins.
3. Refrigerate the pâté for at least an hour.

To serve

1. Slice some pickled cucumber into strips, add some of the reserved mackerel and some dill, and decorate the top of each pâté.
2. Makes 4 tins, 75g per portion.

Seasons
MACKEREL
In Olive Oil
In Olive Oil

WASABI

David Turton, Wasabi Production Manager at The Wasabi Company in Dorchester, Dorset, particularly enjoys the exciting ways in which chefs cook with wasabi

Watercress has been grown on the company's farms since the 1850s. One chef, who visited over a decade ago, remarked how the only other crop he had seen growing in similar conditions was wasabi in Japan. After discovering that it was a difficult crop to grow, and that it had never been successfully grown in Europe, the challenge for growing wasabi was set! "We used some previously abandoned watercress beds and, after a good deal of trial and error, we brought our first wasabi crop to maturity two years later. We still get plenty of surprises from our crops. Harvesting a fully mature plant is always an event, as it's only when you pull the whole plant that you can see what you have yielded," David explains.

Although the vegetable is native to the mountain streams of Japan, The Wasabi Company recreates those conditions in watercress beds with flowing spring water, and now produces fresh wasabi for top chefs in the UK and Europe.

"It's always exciting to see how a chef will choose to use wasabi. It's delicate and loses flavour over time if exposed to high temperatures, so it presents a culinary challenge!"

David continues: "My favourite part of the job is pulling a two-year-old wasabi plant for a visitor to sample here on the farm. Watching their face as the pungency hits their taste buds, followed by the complex flavour is always extremely gratifying."

Award-winning products
2019 – Wasabi Mustard: Gold; Wasabi Mayonnaise: Silver

"It's only when you pull the whole plant that you can see what you have yielded."

Wasabi-seared beef tataki with watercress and cucumber ponzu salad

Recipe by Jaap Schep, Head Chef, The Three Horseshœs, Burton Bradstock, Dorset

Ingredients

600g fillet steak
10g The Watercress Company's Wasabi Mustard
2 bunches of watercress
1 cucumber
1 large shallot
10g fresh ginger
2 cloves of garlic
100ml Japanese rice vinegar
50ml light soy sauce
100g The Watercress Company's Wasabi Mayonnaise
Sesame seeds

To prepare the steak

1. Pan-fry the fillet steak in oil on a very high heat for four to five minutes, turning until brown on all sides, keeping the fillet steak blue/rare.
2. Remove the steak from the pan, then marinate in the wasabi and chill in the fridge.

To prepare the watercress and cucumber salad

1. Wash the watercress in cold water.
2. Cut the cucumber into long, thin strips.

To make the ponzu dressing

1. Finely dice the shallot and add the grated ginger, garlic, rice vinegar and soy sauce.
2. Drizzle over the salad (reserve some for serving).

To serve

1. Thinly slice the fillet steak and fan out onto a plate.
2. Add the watercress salad and drizzle the remaining dressing over.
3. Finish with a few dollops of wasabi mayonnaise and a sprinkling of sesame seeds.

Chef's tip: The steak can be prepared the day before and wrapped tightly in clingfilm. This ensures a round fillet that's easy to slice thinly. If you do this, marinate about 30 minutes before use (not overnight) so that the wasabi retains its distinctive flavour.

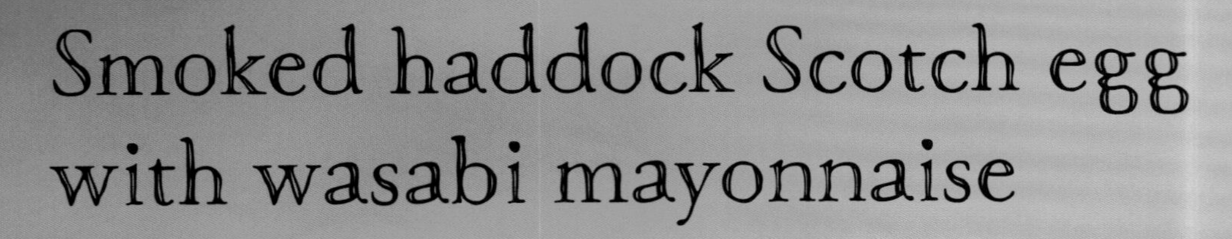

Smoked haddock Scotch egg with wasabi mayonnaise

Recipe by Matt Henderson, Head Chef/Owner, The Victory Inn, St Mawes, Cornwall

Ingredients

For the Scotch eggs
4 medium eggs
1 large skinless smoked haddock, naturally smoked
1 lemon
25g parsley
1 large tbsp of mayonnaise

For the coating
500g panko breadcrumbs
250g flour
100ml milk
1 medium egg

For the wasabi mayonnaise
Fresh wasabi thumb
4 large tbsp of The Watercress Company's Wasabi Mayonnaise

For serving
Salad for dressing the plate

Chef's tip: Buy the eggs a week ahead of when you want to make the Scotch eggs as the shells will be much easier to peel when cooked.

To make the haddock mixture

1. Chop the haddock into small chunks, then finely chop the parsley.
2. Zest and juice the lemon (avoid using the white of the lemon as it can be very bitter).
3. Add the haddock, lemon (zest and juice) and parsley into a blender, blitz on a high speed, until well combined.
4. Remove the mixture and place it into a light tea towel or J-cloth to gently strain any excess moisture.
5. Return to the blender, and add the large tablespoon of mayonnaise, and pulse to combine.
6. Pop this fish mixture into a bowl, then refrigerate until needed.

To make the Scotch eggs

1. Boil the eggs for six minutes (they should be soft in the middle). Cook for longer if you don't like a runny yolk. Drop them into ice-cold water to stop them from cooking.
2. Once cooled, peel carefully as they will be soft.
3. Bring out the fish mixture from the fridge and split into four balls. Carefully flatten the balls and place an egg in the middle, gently wrapping the mixture around the egg. Put back into the fridge to rest.
4. To make the coating: beat an egg and the milk together in a bowl. Fill another bowl with flour and another with the breadcrumbs.
5. Take the eggs out, roll in the flour, followed by the egg mix and finally the breadcrumbs. Leave these to one side.
6. Grate the wasabi and mix into the mayonnaise. Add a small amount to your plates (we like to swipe it across the plate).
7. Heat the oil in a pan to 170°C/150°C fan/gas mark 3. Fry the eggs for six minutes, or until golden brown.

To serve
Place the eggs next to the mayonnaise on the plate and finish with a little salad garnish – watercress works really well.

great taste
fussels
SMOKED
RAPESEED OIL
Mysterious and Aromatic
Extra virgin rapeseed oil
with an oak wood
smoke infusion
250ml ℮

RAPESEED OIL

Andy Fussel, Owner of Fussels Fine Foods in Rode, Somerset, describes how he produces his award-winning oil from the ground up on his farm

"My farm is predominantly an arable farm, although we do grow stubble turnips for a local sheep farmer for grazing and fattening his store lambs. I grow oilseed rape, wheat, barley and maize. From the oilseed rape, I make our award-winning, cold pressed rapeseed oil; it's liquid gold!" explains Andy.

The wheat, barley and maize are mixed and ground for animal feed in the blending shed; while from the oil, Andy makes flavoured oils, salad dressings, mayonnaise, sauce and vinaigrettes. "We grow, harvest, store, press and bottle our rapeseed oil. It is always pressed fresh as it is the seed I store, not the oil. All the oil-based products are produced by hand on my Somerset farm."

In terms of product development, the team comes up with an idea which is then trialled. "We all have a taste, making up a number of options until we find the right one. Sometimes we just know; other times, Lizzy needs to add some tweaking," says Andy.

"Our cold pressed rapeseed oil has a slightly nutty flavour, giving you the best-tasting roasties ever!" enthuses Lizzy Etheridge, who heads up production, tours, sales, events and hospitality at Fussels.

The challenges of farming are a way of life for Andy and his team. "Seeing your produce come to harvest after a weed- and pest-free crop year, resulting in good yields is so satisfying. However, when the cabbage stem flea beetle has eaten 100 acres of my oilseed rape crop, that's a different story!" adds Andy.

Lizzy says that educating people about how Fussels' products are made is an important part of her job. "I love meeting people and sharing my passion for our products. I tell them about the way we farm and use machinery. How we're interested in protecting the bees and wildlife, and maintaining good, nutritious soil to enable our crops to grow well," Lizzy says. It's all part of Fussels' award-winning process.

Award-winning products
2020 – Fussels Cold Pressed Extra Virgin Rapeseed Oil; Fussels Fine Foods Smoked Extra Virgin Rapeseed Oil

Rapeseed oil focaccia

Recipe by Harrison Brockington, Head Chef, Gather, Totnes, Devon

Ingredients
500g bread flour
15g salt
12g yeast
350ml water
75ml Fussels Fine Foods' Cold Pressed Extra Virgin Rapeseed Oil
50g of fresh seaweed, optional

To make the dough

1. Mix the flour and salt together in one bowl, and crumble the yeast into 350ml water in another bowl.
2. Slowly pour the water and yeast combination into the flour, while mixing, to create a dough. Drizzle in 60ml of the oil (reserve the extra 15ml for emulsion) and knead until the dough comes together and is smooth.
3. Cover the dough and allow to prove in a warm space for two hours, or until it has doubled in size.

To cook the bread

1. Add a dash of oil to a tray and pour in the dough to roughly an inch thick.
2. Using your fingertips, spread it out to fill the tray and create some dimples on top.
3. Add a topping: I used local seaweed (sea lettuce and pepper dulce) but rosemary, or sun-dried tomatoes and olives work well too.
4. Allow the dough to prove for another hour, covered.
5. Preheat the oven to 230°C/210°C fan/gas mark 8.
6. Mix 15ml of water with the remaining 15ml of rapeseed oil to form an emulsion and brush this on top of the focaccia.
7. Bake in the oven for 15 minutes, then reduce the temperature to 190°C/180°C fan/gas mark 5 and cook for another 15 minutes.
8. Allow to cool for a further 15 minutes. Enjoy!

Tempura vegetables with sweet chilli and garlic vegan mayonnaise, and rapeseed oil

Recipe by Francesca Moran, Head Chef/Proprietor, Moran's Restaurant & Bar, Westward Ho!, Devon

Ingredients

600g mixed vegetables of your choice, chopped
100g cornflour
150g plain flour
1 tsp turmeric
250ml soda water
280g organic silken tofu
125ml Fussels Fine Foods' Extra Virgin Rapeseed Oil
3 tbsp lime juice
2 tbsp cloudy cider vinegar
Rock salt and pepper
¼ tsp Dijon mustard
2 fresh chillies, sliced
2 cloves of garlic, crushed
2 tbsp of sriracha sauce
Rocket salad leaves (to serve)

To make the mayonnaise

1. Put the tofu, rapeseed oil, lime juice, cloudy cider vinegar, sriracha sauce and mustard in a bowl. Season with rock salt and pepper, and blend until smooth.
2. Grind the chillies and garlic into a paste in a pestle and mortar.
3. Add some paste to the mayonnaise, depending on the desired spice level.

To make the tempura batter

1. Mix 100g of plain flour with all the cornflour and turmeric in a bowl, and then season. Add the soda water and whisk until all the flour has dissolved.
2. Using the remaining 50g of flour, coat the vegetables.
3. Place the vegetables into the batter, ensuring they're completely covered, then carefully fry them in a deep-fat fryer, or pan of oil, at 180 degrees for approximately two to three minutes.
4. Serve on a bed of rocket with the mayonnaise.

Chef's tip: Store any leftover mayonnaise in a sealed container in the fridge for up to five days.

Est
1989
Taste of the West
South West England
GOLD
2020
100% ORGANIC
the original
with the
Ostlers
Raw, unfiltered,
NATURALLY MADE IN DEVON
Est
1989
Taste of the West
South West England
GOLD
2020
100% ORGANIC
the original
with the
mother
Ostlers
ORGANIC APPLE CIDER VINEGAR
Raw, unfiltered, unpasteurised
NATURALLY MADE IN DEVON
WWW.OSTLERSCIDERVINEGAR.COM

CIDER VINEGAR

Rebekah Paterson, Owner of Ostlers Cider Mill in Barnstaple, Devon, proves that hard work pays dividends, as her team demonstrates with award-winning apple cider vinegars

Ostlers makes apple cider vinegar for shops, wholesale customers and chefs, and mainly supplies to the health food industry. The vinegar is sold all over the UK, as well as in Holland and Bangladesh. "We make an award-winning apple cider vinegar, using our own organic orchards to create our vinegar. Ostlers was started back in 1989 when Peter Hartnoll (my father) bought 14 acres of land in Goodleigh, and then planted traditional cider apple trees across the plot – he chose Mitchelins, Browns and Debretts," explains Rebekah.

The business started off as a cider mill, but due to an accident, when a lid came off one of the tanks, it made vinegar. "At this point, my father was in a wheelchair and taking quite a few painkillers for arthritis. A friend told him that it was a lucky accident because cider vinegar was an old Roman remedy for the complaint, so he started to take it. In a few weeks, he was off his painkillers and shortly afterwards, stopped using his wheelchair!" adds Rebekah.

"I came to Ostlers Cider Mill in 2009. It was down a long and bumpy track with orchards planted on very steep slopes which makes them difficult to work. I came to help my father, who was living there without mains electricity, heating or planning permission... just as well I like a challenge," she says.

"I love my life here, and being able to live in the countryside on the farm is a dream come true. It can be tough though. Living off-grid can have its moments. In winter, when the generator breaks down and I'm left with no electricity, or when we're all soggy and fed up during the harvest in November and the pressing machinery breaks down... I have many stories," continues Rebekah.

Her hard work has paid off however. "I feel very proud when a customer tells me how much our vinegar has helped them with all sorts of medical problems, or simply seeing someone put our vinegar into their shopping trolley. One of the proudest moments has to be receiving Best of Sauces & Accompaniments in 2012 at the Taste of the West Awards at the Eden Project. It was the first year we entered, and I was completely blown away with the judges' comments, and how well we did." Rebekah and her team definitely have a winning formula, as Ostlers keeps on winning awards!

Award-winning products
2019 – Cloudy Cider Vinegar: Gold
2020 – Cloudy Cider Vinegar: Gold; Organic Cider Vinegar: Gold

Apple, celeriac and red cabbage coleslaw

Recipe by Joe Nagy, Head Chef, Lordleaze Hotel, Chard, Somerset

Ingredients

100g carrots (peeled, topped and tailed)
200g red cabbage
200g celeriac
50g red onion
50g white onion
1 clove of garlic, crushed to a paste
2 Granny Smith apples, unpeeled
150ml Ostlers Organic Apple Cider Vinegar
100g caster sugar
200ml mayonnaise
Salt and pepper

Method

1. Grate the carrots, and thinly slice the red cabbage, celeriac and onions, then add the vinegar and sugar. Season and leave to marinate for 10–15 minutes.
2. Add the garlic.
3. Grate the apple, add to the bowl, and mix all the above together.
4. Add the mayonnaise and stir through to bind the vegetables.

Chef's tip: You could add a splash more vinegar for acidity.

Cider vinegar roasted pork belly on an Asian apple cabbage salad with tamarind sauce

Recipe by Francesca Moran, Head Chef/Proprietor,
Moran's Restaurant & Bar, Westward Ho!, Devon

Ingredients

800g pork belly
2 carrots, sliced
1 carrot, grated
2 shallots, sliced
Rapeseed oil (for the skin and for frying)
500ml boiling water
2 tsp chicken bouillon
6 tsp Ostlers Cloudy Apple Cider Vinegar
Rock salt
130g tamarind paste
2 tsp fish sauce
130g sugar
400ml water
½ tsp salt
3 tbsp tomato ketchup
1 tbsp sriracha
¼ red cabbage, thinly sliced
¼ white cabbage, thinly sliced
1 red onion, thinly sliced
1 white onion, thinly sliced
1 red apple, thinly sliced
Spring onion, sliced (for garnish)
Sesame seeds (optional)
Crispy fried onion (optional)

To cook the pork

1. Preheat the oven to 220°C/200°C fan/gas mark 7.
2. Place the pork belly in a pan of water and bring to the boil. Simmer for about five minutes, then drain and transfer to a board and pat dry.
3. Score the skin diagonally to create a criss-cross, leave to air dry, then massage in some rapeseed oil and rock salt.
4. Put the shallots and sliced carrots into a roasting tray with the pork belly on top, skin-side up.
5. Mix the bouillon and vinegar with the water and pour into the tray (nearly up to the level of the skin), but make sure the skin is kept dry.
6. Place in the centre of the oven and cook until the skin is nice and crispy, for about 90 minutes, rotating the tray halfway through the cooking process.
7. When cooked, transfer the pork to a tray, allow to cool, then refrigerate. When cold, slice the pork, skin-side down on the board into portions.
8. Mix the white and red cabbage, half of the red and white onions, the grated carrot and apple into a bowl, then turn out onto a plate.
9. Heat a couple of dashes of rapeseed oil in a wok, add the sliced pork belly, the remaining red and white onion and stir for a minute.
10. Add the tamarind paste, sugar, salt, fish sauce, tomato ketchup and sriracha, then stir in some water to loosen. Cook until the sauce reduces, making sure the pork belly is coated.

To serve

Place the pork belly on top of the cabbage salad, garnish with some crispy fried onion, spring onion and sesame seeds.

Atjar tjampœr (Indonesian sweet and sour pickled vegetables)

Recipe by Jaap Schep, Head Chef, The Three Horseshœs, Burton Bradstock, Dorset

Ingredients

500g white cabbage
2 carrots
2 red peppers
1 bunch of spring onions
2 red onions
300ml Ostlers Organic Apple Cider Vinegar
200ml water
200g sugar
A large piece of ginger
2 cloves of garlic
2 red chillies
5g ground turmeric
1 small bunch of coriander

Method

1. In a pan, bring the vinegar, water and sugar to the boil.
2. Roughly chop the ginger, garlic and chillies and add to the liquid. Then add the turmeric and simmer for around 10 minutes.
3. Finely shred the white cabbage and place in a large bowl. Grate and add the carrots, then finely slice the red peppers, red onions and spring onions and add those to the bowl too.
4. Taste the pickling liquid and add more sugar or vinegar, depending on your taste.
5. Remove the ginger, garlic and red chillies.
6. Add the liquid to the bowl of vegetables.
7. Finely chop the coriander and add to the bowl.
8. Sterilise some Kilner jars, fill them with the pickled vegetables and store in a cool and dark cupboard for up to six months.

Chef's tip: Pickled vegetables work alongside many dishes – their sharp acidity complements all meats and cheeses too.

Victory's Bloody Mary with Cornishman's Relish

Recipe by Matt Henderson, Head Chef/Owner, The Victory Inn, St Mawes, Cornwall

Ingredients

2 large handfuls of ice
200ml vodka
600ml tomato juice
2 tbsp lemon juice (plus 4 slices to serve)
1 large tsp of Deli Farm Charcuterie's Cornishman's Relish
4 tbsp Tabasco sauce
4 tbsp Worcestershire sauce
Pinch of sea salt
Pinch of black pepper
4 celery sticks (to serve)

Method

1. Place the ice into four glasses.
2. Measure out the vodka, tomato juice, lemon juice, Cornishman's Relish, Tabasco and Worcestershire sauce, and put in a blender.
3. Blitz together until mixed, then pour evenly into each glass over the ice.
4. Season each one with a little sea salt and black pepper.
5. Serve with a slice of lemon and a celery stick.

"It's a unique crop grown in
mineral-rich spring water…
so clean you can drink it!"

WATERCRESS

Luke Beech, Watercress Production Manager at The Watercress Company in Dorchester, Dorset, tells us how he grows his award-winning super salad leaves

Luke, quite simply, sums up his produce as "wonderful watercress grown in deepest Dorset". He describes the process: "We grow healthy and delicious watercress. It's a unique crop grown in mineral-rich spring water... so clean you can drink it! While we use gravel-lined beds to grow our crops in traditional ways, they are produced to the highest modern technical standards."

The Watercress Company's leaves are enjoyed by chefs and diners across the South West. It supplies a growing number of local and national distributors with baby leaf, watercress and fresh wasabi in a range of punnets, bags and trays. As specialists in niche crops, it ensures that the finest quality baby leaf and watercress are harvested daily – when they are at their very best. "It never ceases to amaze us what the talented chefs in the South West can create with our produce," Luke adds.

What are the challenges facing this team of growers? "It has to be the weather, full stop. My job is pretty hard to beat when the sun is shining in the early morning in the middle of a British summer, but when we are preparing the beds over winter with everything January can throw at us, summer seems a long way off!"

Luke continues: "Over the last two winters, the team and I have been working to rebuild the Dorset watercress beds. It's hard work and a tricky process to get right. When we do, and we see the first crops coming through that are perfectly uniform, with a lovely, table-top even level, I get a huge sense of pride and achievement and know that all our hard work has been worth it."

Award-winning products
2020 – Watercress Pesto: Gold

Watercress soup with poached egg and crispy onions

Recipe by Matt Henderson, Head Chef/Owner, The Victory Inn, St Mawes, Cornwall

Ingredients

For the soup
500g of The Watercress Company's Watercress
1 vegetable stock cube
500ml water
1 onion
4 cloves of garlic, grated
1 small stick of celery
Salt and pepper
Oil for frying

For the eggs
300ml water
30ml white wine vinegar
4 eggs
Cold water

To serve
50g crispy onions

To make the soup

1. Heat the oil in a large saucepan. Add the onion, celery and garlic, and sweat until soft, for approximately five minutes.
2. Boil the water in a separate saucepan, add the vegetable stock cube and let it dissolve.
3. Once the vegetables have softened, add the vegetable stock to this pan, reduce the heat and simmer for five minutes.
4. Then add the watercress to the liquid, season and simmer for another two minutes. It's important you don't leave the watercress to boil away, as it can turn the soup brown and lose its vibrant green colour.
5. Once done, blend the soup and keep it warm.

To make the eggs

1. Add the water for the eggs into another saucepan, along with the vinegar and bring to a rolling simmer.
2. Crack the eggs into separate ramekins or bowls. This helps keep their shape.
3. When the water is bubbling, spin it with a spoon so that it's swirling, then drop the eggs in one by one and cook for three and a half minutes. They should be slightly soft to touch with a runny yolk.
4. Place them in cold water to stop the cooking process.

To serve

Ladle the soup into four bowls, place the poached eggs on top and sprinkle over some crispy onions.

CHEESE

Peter Morgan, owner of The Book and Bucket Cheese Company in Cranborne, Dorset, crafts his cheeses using traditional methods and local, seasonal ingredients

When I first started making cheese, I sought the advice of people that had between them over 120 years of experience in the industry. They said the starting point was to buy some books and read as much as possible; after that, it is just "bucket science"!

In January 2019, with a decade of dairy industry experience, my bucket-full of recipes and ideas came together and The Book and Bucket Cheese Company was born, named in recognition of where the journey started. "In keeping with the theme, our cheeses are all named after authors, from Hardy's to Shakespeare, Burns to Hemingway," adds Peter.

These can be found throughout the region and beyond, in delis, farm shops and on menus of restaurants and pubs.

"Our products have been crafted to appeal to most cheeseboards and menus, at any time of the year. We're inspired by what's around us as well as the seasons," explains Peter. "We have soft cheese made with local wild garlic for the spring, feta and halloumi for summer salads and BBQs, as well as a cheeseboard brie selection, a matured Manchego, a creamy blue, and a soft cheese that we top with pink peppercorns or edible flowers," adds Peter. "I want people to fall in love with our take on their favourite cheese, then be inspired with the rest of our range."
"We start the same way every day: radio on, coffee on, 20 minutes setting the world to rights while waiting for the vats to heat up, then bring on the cheesemaking!"

All our cheese is pasteurised and only vegetarian rennet is used. "Once the milk is ready, a chosen blend of cultures is added for that particular product, and then we let science do its thing (time for that second cup of coffee). Next, rennet is added to set the milk, before it's cut to separate the curds and whey," Peter explains.

The detail at each stage is key. The curds need to be at the correct temperature, cut to the right size, and at the right acidity to make the perfect cheese. It's then moulded and left to rest, this can be for an hour, or two days, depending on the type. "Some cheese can be eaten on the same day, others take up to two years before they are ready to eat," Peter adds.

Award-winning products
2020 – Shakespeare Sheep Milk Cheese: Gold; Hemingway Cheese, Kalamata Brine Matured Feta: Gold; Hardy's: Gold; Smokey Burns, Gold

Mussels cooked in beer with brie and beer bread

Recipe by Joe Nagy, Head Chef, Lordleaze Hotel, Chard, Somerset

Ingredients

2 lb mussels (in shells)
1 tbsp olive oil
4 sprigs of thyme
3 cloves of garlic, minced
¼ tsp chilli flakes
2 large shallots, chopped
Freshly ground black pepper
½ pint of Palmers Dorset Gold
1–3 tbsp butter, to taste
1 tbsp fresh tarragon/parsley, chopped
100g The Book and Bucket's Shakespeare White Bloom Rind Cheese

Method

1. Rinse the mussels under cold running water, and clean them using a sharp knife or your fingers to pull off the beards.
2. In a soup pot with a tight-fitting cover, heat the olive oil, then add the thyme, garlic, chilli, shallots, and a pinch of salt and pepper. Sauté for three minutes.
3. Pour in the beer and simmer.
4. Add the mussels and cover, allowing the mussels to steam, stirring once or twice, until they open.
5. Use a slotted spoon to transfer the mussels into bowls. Discard any that have not opened.
6. Add the butter, herbs and brie to the pan juices, and boil, whisking until the butter melts.
7. Pour over the mussels, and serve with some of the crusty beer bread (see page 114 for recipe).

Sheep's cheese and Serrano ham croquettes with sun-blush tomato sauce

Recipe by Jaap Schep, Head Chef, The Three Horseshoes, Burton Bradstock, Dorset

Ingredients

150g The Book and Bucket's Shakespeare Sheep Milk Cheese, grated
6 slices Serrano ham
100g butter
190g plain flour
500ml semi-skimmed milk
1 tsp mustard
2 tbsp flat-leaf parsley, finely chopped
100g sun-blushed tomatoes
100g panko breadcrumbs
2 eggs
Salt and pepper
100g mayonnaise

Chef's tip: This dish works just as well without the ham as a delicious vegetarian starter.

Method

1. Melt the butter in a pan over a medium heat, add 120g of the flour and cook for one minute.
2. Add the milk, whisk until smooth, then reduce the heat and cook gently for three minutes until the sauce has thickened, stirring constantly.
3. Add the chopped parsley, mustard and 50g of the tomatoes.
4. Remove the mixture from the heat and add the grated cheese.
5. Finely slice the ham into strips and add to the mixture.
6. Season with salt and pepper, then refrigerate the mixture for at least two hours.
7. To make the croquettes, shape the thick, chilled sauce into the size of small golf balls.
8. Beat the eggs in a shallow bowl and put 70g of the flour on a plate.
9. Roll the balls in the flour, then in the egg, before coating in the breadcrumbs.
10. Mix the mayonnaise with the remaining 50g of sun-blushed tomatoes (finely chopped).
11. Heat some oil for deep-frying to 180°C/165°C fan/gas mark 4. Drop the croquettes into the oil, and cook for one to two minutes, until crisp and golden.

To serve

Drain on a kitchen towel and serve with the sun-blushed tomato mayonnaise.

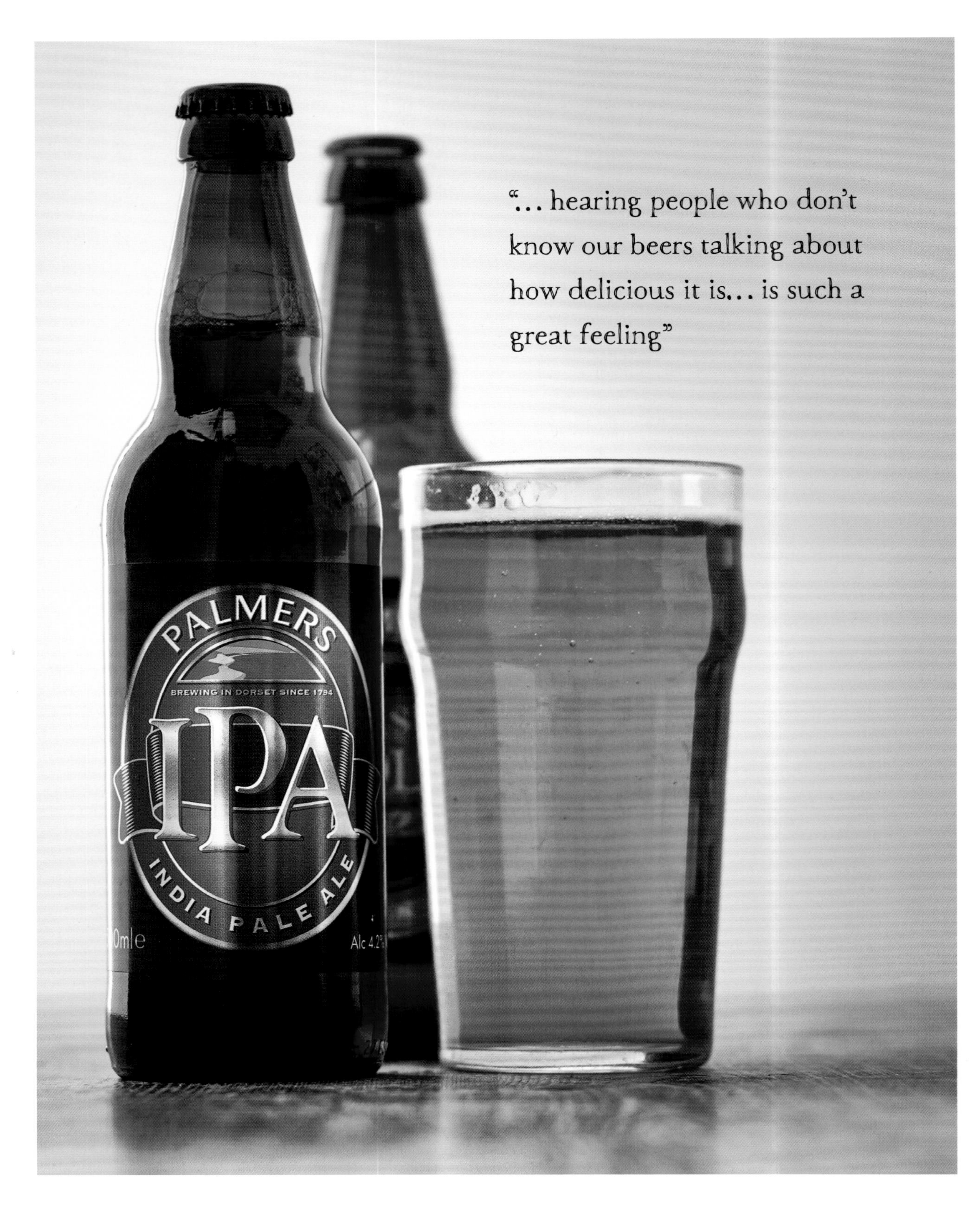

"... hearing people who don't know our beers talking about how delicious it is... is such a great feeling"

BEER

Darren Batten, Head Brewer and Director of Palmers Brewery in Bridport, Dorset, talks about his company's success and the enjoyment of his job

Palmers Brewery, established in 1794, is family-owned and brews cask ales as well as a keg 'craft ale'. The brewing process hasn't changed in over 200 years and it takes place in a traditional brewhouse with no automation. Palmers also owns 53 tenanted pubs in Devon, Dorset and Somerset.

"We are, in fact, the only thatched brewery in the UK, and one of the prettiest," Darren says.

How does the team at Palmers keep things fresh? "New recipes start with a conversation with my senior team. Basically, the MD says 'brew me something new and different'. After a discussion, we then decide how strong, what colour, how bitter and what aroma? It's left to me to create the first brew and get it right first time. The smallest quantity we can brew is 8,500 pints, so it's a bit of a challenge! To be honest, however the beer turns out, I have the advantage of saying 'that's exactly how I wanted it to taste' as the rest of my team know a lot less than me about brewing," laughs Darren.

The brewery supplies Palmers' beer to its own pubs, as well as bars, pubs, restaurants, wine shops and farm shops across the south of England. "Basically from West Devon to London and the south coast up to around the M4," Darren explains.

"Standing in a pub drinking a cask ale that I brewed, and hearing people who don't know our beers talking about how delicious it is, as they taste their first pint of Palmers, is such a great feeling," enthuses Darren. "However, getting up on a cold, wet, dark and dreary winter's morning, and having to be in the brewhouse at 6.45am to 'mash-in' isn't great. Although this improves quickly, when I hug a warm mash tun and breathe in the rich aroma of brewing!"

"I've had many proud moments in my 29 years at Palmers. Developing our first-ever seasonal ale (Colmers), and drinking that first pint in a pub was pretty special. And also winning SIBA South West Champion Cask Ale 2019 with Tally Ho was really satisfying. In the current world – where there are so many new brewers – this was a massive accolade for all of us."

Award-winning products
2019 – Palmers 200, Palmers Tally Ho!: Gold; Palmers Dorset Gold: Silver; Palmers IPA: Commended
2020 – Palmers IPA (500ml bottle), Palmers Tally Ho! (500ml bottle): Gold; Dorset Gold (500ml bottle): Silver

Beer bread

Recipe by Joe Nagy, Head Chef, Lordleaze Hotel, Chard, Somerset

Ingredients

3 cups flour (sifted)
3 tsp baking powder (omit if using self-raising flour)
1 tsp salt (omit if using self-raising flour)
¼ cup sugar
1 (12oz) bottle of Palmers Dorset Gold
½ cup melted butter (¼ cup will do just fine)

Method

1. Preheat the oven to 190°C/ 170°C fan/gas mark 5.
2. Mix the dry ingredients together and then add the beer.
3. Pour into a greased loaf pan.
4. Pour the melted butter over the mixture.
5. Bake for one hour, remove from pan and cool for at least 15 minutes.

Chef's tips: This recipe makes a very hearty bread with a crunchy, buttery crust. If you prefer a softer crust (like a traditional bread), mix the butter into the batter instead of pouring it over the top.

Sifting flour for bread recipes is a must-do. Most people just scoop the cup measure in the flour canister and level it off. That compacts the flour and will turn your bread into a 'hard biscuit'. Try it once the correct way and you will see an amazing difference in the end product.

Ale-marinated venison medallions with champ mash, buttered kale, braised baby carrots and rich ale jus

Recipe by Owen Isaacs, Executive Head Chef, The Grand Hotel, Torquay, Devon

Ingredients

200g venison loin
1 bottle of Palmers Tally Ho! Ale
2 large banana shallots, finely chopped
2 large Maris Piper potatoes, cooked and mashed
2 spring onions, chopped
200ml venison stock, reduced (pre-made for the jus)
50g redcurrant jelly
1 sprig of rosemary
2 cloves of garlic
80g butter, unsalted
Vegetable oil
Salt and pepper
Watercress sprigs (for garnish)
Kale, baby carrots, asparagus (enough to serve four)
Carrot purée (enough to serve four)

To prepare the meat

1. Trim the venison loin (or ask the butcher to trim it for you) and marinate in the ale for 24 hours.

To cook the dish

1. Pan-fry the shallots for a few minutes, until golden.
2. Add the venison stock and ale marinade to the shallots, and gently reduce the liquid. This should take around 20 minutes.
3. Add the redcurrant jelly and reduce for a further five minutes.
4. Cut the venison into medallions and pan-fry with the rosemary and garlic over a medium-hot heat, for three to five minutes on each side (for medium rare). Set aside to rest.
5. Heat the mashed potato in a separate pan and add the chopped spring onions. Heat until the onion is cooked, and then season.
6. Warm a plate in the oven.
7. Sauté all the vegetables in 25g of butter for a few minutes, then arrange them onto the plate.
8. Place the venison on the mash champ.
9. Add the remaining 55g of butter to the stock and simmer until there is a sheen. Pour a little around the venison.
10. Garnish with the watercress and carrot purée to finish.

"We have a really interesting orchard with over 458 different varieties of apples – a dream for our cider makers."

CIDER

Eleanor Thatcher, a fifth-generation Cider Maker at Thatchers Cider in Sandford, Somerset, is passionate about her business. Here, she describes the year-round dedication needed to produce award-winning drinks

This family company makes a range of Somerset ciders from its home at Myrtle Farm. "This includes a speciality Cider Barn range and our bestselling Thatchers Gold and Haze ciders. We've just introduced a Cloudy Lemon cider and Thatchers Zero – our first alcohol-free cider," says Eleanor.

"Out in the orchards, we've got a farm team dedicated to caring for the apples all year round. It's important to us that only the highest quality fruit goes through our mill and into our ciders. At harvest, which runs from the end of August to November, we like to get the apples pressed within 24 hours of leaving the orchard, to retain the luscious, fruity flavours. The extracted juice is then carefully fermented – combined with yeast to create alcohol – and it's this special process that really brings out the best of the flavour. After fermentation, the juice is matured and blended, then packaged." Thatchers' ciders are found in pubs across the UK, supermarkets, independents and farm shops.

The team loves trialling new apple varieties, or combinations of varieties. "We've got a small pilot plant at the farm, where our cider makers can create small runs of new cider styles for testing. We have a really interesting orchard with over 458 different varieties of apples – a dream for our cider makers. We're after two main things: a cider that is excellent quality, and one that is going to be enjoyed by our customers," Eleanor explains.

Eleanor embraces her farming lifestyle. "I love getting out onto the farm when the blossom is out and the bees are buzzing. I also like tasting our ciders – there is something magical about the fermentation process of turning apple juice into cider." She concludes: "It makes me really proud to see something we have produced being enjoyed by others. I also find it exciting when we launch a new product. It's so satisfying to see it moving along the production line for the first time."

Award-winning products
2019 – Thatchers Rascal: Silver; Thatchers Rose: Commended
2020 – Thatchers Katy, Thatchers Zero: Gold; Thatchers Rascal: Silver; Thatchers Rosé: Commended

Pork tenderloin with sweet cider sauce, pomme purée, baby carrots, sautéed spinach, braised apple rings and cream cider jus

Recipe by Owen Isaacs, Executive Head Chef, The Grand Hotel, Torquay, Devon

Ingredients

200g pork tenderloin
2 bottles of Thatchers Rascal Cider
2 large banana shallots, finely chopped
2 large Maris Piper potatoes, mashed (enough for four)
180ml veal stock reduction (pre-made for jus)
160ml double cream
1 red apple
2 cloves of garlic
1 sprig of rosemary
80g butter, unsalted
2 tsp wholegrain mustard
Vegetable oil
Salt and pepper
Watercress sprigs (for garnish)
Spinach (enough for four)
Baby carrots (enough for four)
Apple sauce (for serving)

To prepare the meat

Marinate the pork in a bottle of the cider for 24 hours.

To cook the dish

1. Preheat the oven to 180°C/160°C fan/gas mark 4.
2. Fry the shallots in a pan for a few minutes until golden.
3. Add the stock, a glug or two of cider, and simmer to reduce for 20 minutes.
4. Add the double cream, and simmer to reduce for a further five minutes, then set aside.
5. Pan-fry the pork with the rosemary and garlic on both sides to sear the meat.
6. Place the pork in the oven to finish cooking for about 10 minutes, then set aside to rest.
7. Core and slice the apple into rings and sauté with another glug or two of cider to coat them, and leave to infuse.
8. Heat the mashed potato in a separate pan, and season.
9. Sauté all the vegetables in butter, then arrange them on a plate and keep hot.
10. Slice the pork into three, place on top of the mash with the apple rings.
11. Return the cider cream to the heat, add the butter and mustard to thicken.
12. Circle the dish with the cider cream, garnish with a sprig of watercress and serve with the apple sauce.

Spiced Somerset apple, sultana, walnut and cider cake with custard

Recipe by Joe Nagy, Head Chef, Lordleaze Hotel, Chard, Somerset

Ingredients
175g sultanas
150ml Thatchers Rascal Cider
280g self-raising flour
1½ tsp baking powder
1 tsp ground cinnamon
1 tsp ground coriander
1 pinch of salt
225g unrefined caster sugar
180g unsalted butter
2 medium eggs
Zest of 1 lemon
50g chopped walnuts (pecans also work well)
2 large cooking apples, peeled and cored
2 Granny Smith apples, peeled and cored
2 tsp brandy
1 tbsp demerara sugar

For the custard
4 cups whole milk
1 tbsp vanilla extract
1 tsp butter
4 eggs
½ cup white sugar
3 tbsp cornstarch

To make the cake
1. Set the oven to 170°C/150°C fan/gas mark 3.
2. Butter or oil spray a 20cm round cake tin and line the base with a disc of baking parchment.
3. Warm the cider a little and soak the sultanas in it for about 20 minutes.
4. Finely slice the cooking apples, dribble over the brandy and toss well.
5. Sieve the flour, baking powder, salt, cinnamon and coriander into a bowl.
6. Cream the sugar and butter for about five minutes, until pale and fluffy, then beat in the eggs a little at a time.
7. Fold in the dry ingredients and the chopped walnuts (or pecans), followed by the lemon zest and apples.
8. Stir in the soaked sultanas, along with any remaining cider.
9. Spoon the mixture into the prepared tin, level off, sprinkle with the demerara sugar and bake for 45–50 minutes, or until a skewer comes out clean.
10. Cool in the tin, then on a wire rack until completely cold.

To make the custard
1. Add the milk, vanilla extract and butter to a saucepan on a medium heat, keep stirring until simmering. Remove the mixture from the heat before it reaches boiling point.
2. Whisk the eggs, white sugar and cornstarch together in a bowl until the sugar dissolves.
3. Put the saucepan back over a low heat. Slowly pour in the egg mixture, whisking constantly, until the custard thickens enough to coat the bottom of a spoon. This will take between five and ten minutes.

"Our story is rooted in a botanical heritage. We draw together a wealth of knowledge and experience, along with an intense curiosity for the unusual!"

What makes an award-winning gin? Ros Nelmes, Master Creator of Fordington Gin in Dorchester, Dorset, has the answers

Fordington Gin supplies mainly independent, artisan food outlets, farm shops and wine merchants throughout the South West.

Gurt Lush is a luxury, local gin, crafted at home by Fordington Gin in possibly the smallest gin house in England. Dorset has some of the most exceptional produce in the country, making it the perfect home for this company.

Ros explains: "Our story is rooted in a botanical heritage. We draw together a wealth of knowledge and experience, along with an intense curiosity for the unusual, which resonates perfectly with our Gurt Lush gin. Handcrafted by us, it's bold and unique – Gurt Lush is seafaring strength, made with Fordington's magical twist."

Ros says that the background to her success story comes from a love of food and flavours. "I am always seeking out something new, inspiring and creative. Fordington Gin has evolved from this knowledge and experience, and we are very proud of what we have achieved!"

Gurt Lush is created with a unique combination of carefully sourced botanicals (organic where possible) and uses only English-grown wheat as its base spirit. "Our gin has a gentle and distinctive flavour which comes from using juniper, mint, fennel and lemon balm," Ros explains.

Winning a number of prestigious awards are her proudest moments to date. Gurt Lush has won gold twice at the Taste of the West, as well as two international gold awards. "We were shortlisted by Raymond Blanc and won silver at the World Gin Awards competing against 600 other gins, and were recognised for our commitment to the community during the pandemic," she adds.

"Real excitement comes from discovering perfect combinations and garnishes to add to our gin. The food pairing side is also fantastic! We love our gin – and very much hope you do too."

Award-winning products
2019 – Gurt Lush Gin: Gold; Fordington Gin: Commended
2020 – Gurt Lush Gin: Gold

Cocktail: Totnes 75

Recipe by Harrison Brockington, Head Chef, Gather, Totnes, Devon

Ingredients

1 tsp honey
25ml Gurt Lush from Fordington Gin
25ml homemade sorrel juice (Granny Smith apple and sorrel)
Champagne, or dry sparkling wine
Ice
1 sorrel leaf (to garnish)

Method

1. To make the homemade sorrel juice: juice one Granny Smith apple with a handful of sorrel, and strain through a cloth.
2. Pour the honey, gin and sorrel juice into a cocktail shaker, then fill it up with ice.
3. Shake well, then strain into a champagne flute.
4. Top up with champagne, swirl gently with a cocktail stirrer, and garnish with a sorrel leaf.

Chef's tip: This cocktail is light, summery and perfect for a celebration or as an aperitif. The gin's fennel fragrance complements the sorrel's green apple flavour.

25ml
50ml

Gin and blood orange granita

Recipe by Jaap Schep, Head Chef, The Three Horseshoes, Burton Bradstock, Dorset

Ingredients

For the granita
100ml water
200g sugar
100ml Gurt Lush Fordington Gin
500ml lemon tonic water
2 blood oranges
1 pomegranate
Fresh mint

For the meringues
2 large egg whites
100g caster sugar
Food colouring

To make the granita

1. Bring the water and the sugar to a boil, then simmer for two minutes.
2. Zest and juice the oranges.
3. Add the gin, orange zest and juice to the water syrup and pour into a freezer-proof container.
4. Cool to room temperature, then freeze for two hours, whisking after the first and second hour.
5. Before serving, break up the granita with a fork to give it a soft texture.

To make the meringues

1. Preheat the oven to 110°C/100°C fan/gas mark ¼ and line a tray with non-stick baking paper.
2. In a large bowl, beat the egg whites until stiff, then gradually beat in the caster sugar until smooth.
3. With a small brush, paint the inside of a piping bag with three long stripes of food colouring.
4. Fill the piping bag with the meringue mixture, and pipe onto the baking tray in any shape you like.
5. Place in the preheated oven and cook for two hours, then leave to cool.

To serve
Place some granita in a stemmed glass, topped with pomegranate seeds, meringues and fresh mint.

Chef's tip: Gurt Lush Fordington Gin is 50% abv. If you use classic gin (40%), increase the amount to 125ml.

"Our process allows us to make a consistently perfect, tongue-tickling curd with lovely, nibbly bits of zest."

LEMON CURD

Charlie Beeden, owner of Beeden & Beeden in Winsford, Minehead, Somerset, is a small producer whose lemon curd has met with great success

Beeden & Beeden is probably one of the smallest producers you are likely to encounter. One half of the Beeden duo is Charlie, maker and chief washer-upper. The other is Zara – taster, labeller and putter-on of TOTW award stickers!

"We started making lemon curd years ago at Zara's mother's request, using her recipe. Several people tried it and asked for more, so we made it for them. We then tweaked the recipe until we got to where we are today – an award-winning product. What could be better than that?" says Charlie.

From their Exmoor kitchen, Charlie and Zara make very small batches of lemon curd, strictly to order, supplying a few specialist local delis. "That said," Charlie adds, "our curd has also been enjoyed in Paris, London, Madeira and Sri Lanka, and has made forays into Cornwall, Hampshire and East Sussex. We guess we're a bit exclusive – it's a funny old world!"

Why do people like it? "We are such a tiny enterprise, so are genuinely homemade. We select fresh lemons ourselves from the local greengrocer. We use the juice and zest, butter, free-range eggs and sugar – that's it. Our process allows us to make a consistently perfect, tongue-tickling curd with lovely, nibbly bits of zest," Charlie explains.

Charlie and Zara discovered that their curd didn't change character when used in the Lemon Bakewell recipe for this book. "Sara from Sara's Petite Cuisine's excellent Bakewell is testament to her brilliant cooking, and echoes the fact that our product still tastes just like it does on the spoon. Who knew it would go so well with almond?"

Award-winning products
2019 – Beeden & Beeden Lemon Curd: Gold

Lemon curd Bakewell

Recipe by Sara Felix, Owner, Sara's Petite Cuisine, Topsham, Devon

Ingredients

For the pastry
250g plain flour
125g very cold butter, unsalted
4 tbsp cold water
Pinch of salt
1 egg yolk

For the filling
150g ground almonds
150g butter, unsalted
150g caster sugar
30g plain flour
2 eggs
1 tbsp almond extract
150g Beeden & Beeden's Lemon Curd

For the icing
300g icing sugar
1 tsp almond paste
Yellow food colouring
Water

To make and cook the pastry
1. Sieve the flour into a bowl, then rub in the butter, followed by a pinch of salt.
2. Add the egg yolk and water, and mix until a dough is formed.
3. Roll the dough out on a lightly floured surface so that it will line a 25cm tart tin (a loose-based tin is preferable).
4. Refrigerate for 30 minutes.
5. Heat the oven to 180°C.
6. Blind bake the pastry case for 15 minutes by placing a sheet of parchment paper over some baking beans that sit on top of the pastry.
7. Remove the parchment paper and baking beans and cook for a further 10 minutes, or until the pastry is dry and light gold in colour.
8. Remove from the oven and leave to cool.

To make the filling
1. Beat the sugar and butter together until light and airy.
2. Add the eggs one at a time, followed by the flour, then fold in the almonds and almond extract.
3. Spread the lemon curd over the base of the pastry case, then pipe the almond filling on top to avoid lemon curd mixing with the filling.
4. Bake the tart for 40 to 45 minutes at 180°C, until the frangipane is firm and golden on top.
5. Cool before icing.

To make the icing
1. Sieve the icing sugar into a bowl, mix in the almond paste and add the water – tablespoon by tablespoon – until a smooth paste is formed.
2. Place three tablespoons into a spare bowl and add a little yellow food colouring – enough to make a lemon-yellow icing. Spoon this yellow icing into a small piping bag with a plain nozzle (or no nozzle and snip the end).
3. Spoon the white icing on top of the tart, spreading all over to form a smooth surface.
4. Pipe parallel lines of yellow icing over the white icing, then drag a cocktail stick through the lines to create a feathered effect.
5. Leave it to set, and enjoy.

Lemon curd Paris-Brest, white chocolate, raspberries and pistachios

Recipe by Matthew Street, Executive Chef,

The Eastbury Hotel & Spa, Seasons Restaurant, Sherborne, Dorset

Ingredients

For the Paris-Brest buns
40g plain flour
25g unsalted butter
1 large egg, beaten
1 egg yolk, beaten
75ml water

For the white chocolate mascarpone
60ml double cream
125g mascarpone
100g white chocolate

To fill
Beeden & Beeden's Lemon Curd
Fresh raspberries
Handful of white chocolate, chopped
Handful of pistachios, chopped

To top
Chopped pistachios
Freeze-dried raspberries
Apricot jam
Icing sugar (to sprinkle)

Method

1 Preheat the oven to 220°C/200°C fan/gas mark 7.
2 Line a tray with baking paper and draw a 10cm circle in the middle. Turn the paper over so the pencil marks face down.

To make the white chocolate filling

1 Warm the double cream, remove from the heat and fold in the white chocolate until melted, then add the mascarpone until all is combined. Be careful not to overwork this.
2 Put the mixture into a piping bag and store in the fridge for later.

To make the Paris-Brest

1 Sift the flour straight onto a piece of baking paper.
2 Place the butter and water into a small saucepan over a low heat, until the butter is melted.
3 Bring to the boil and immediately remove from the heat.
4 Tip the flour in and beat vigorously with a wooden spoon until the dough comes away from the sides of the pan.
5 Allow to cool slightly, then gradually beat in the egg until the dough is smooth and glossy.
6 Spoon the dough into a piping bag and snip off the tip to make a generous-sized hole.
7 Pipe a thick ring onto the circle of the baking paper. Brush with the egg yolk. Stick down the corners of the baking paper using any leftover dough (this will prevent the paper from curling up in the oven).

Continued on page 136

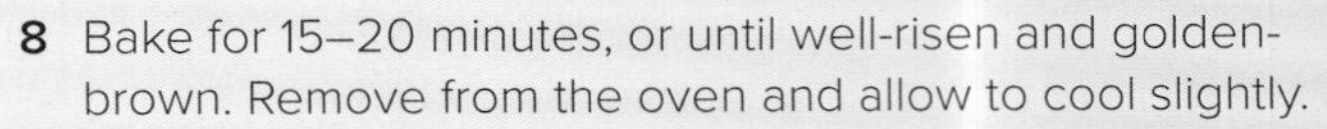

8 Bake for 15–20 minutes, or until well-risen and golden-brown. Remove from the oven and allow to cool slightly.

9 Slice the ring in half, horizontally. It should be soft in the centre and slightly crisp on the outside (dry it out in the residual heat of the oven if necessary).

10 Warm a tablespoon of apricot jam with a teaspoon of water to make a glaze and brush the top of the choux buns with it to glue the pistachios and raspberries on top.

11 Fill the choux rings with the curd, raspberries, white chocolate and pistachios, and sprinkle the buns with icing sugar.

Floating lemon clouds with lemon curd custard

Recipe by Owen Isaacs, Executive Head Chef, The Grand Hotel, Torquay, Devon

Ingredients

For the lemon custard
5 egg yolks
450ml milk
50g caster sugar
1 tbsp cornflour
½ tsp vanilla essence
2 tbsp lemon juice
Half a lemon rind, grated
4 tbsp fromage frais

For the lemon clouds
2 egg whites
4 tbsp caster sugar

For serving
Beeden & Beeden's Lemon Curd
Handful of fresh strawberries
4 strips of candied lemon peel
4 sprigs of mint

Chef's tip: Leave plenty of room between the 'clouds' in the frying pan when poaching, as they swell considerably.

To make the lemon custard

1. Put the egg yolks, milk, caster sugar and cornflour into a saucepan and heat gently, stirring constantly until the custard has thickened. Remove from the heat.
2. Stir in the vanilla essence, lemon juice and rind, and leave to cool.
3. Once cool, stir in the fromage frais until well blended, then refrigerate.

To make and poach the lemon clouds

1. Whisk the egg whites until they become soft peaks, then gradually add in the caster sugar, and continue whisking until stiff.
2. Bring some water to a gentle simmer in a frying pan.
3. Using a tablespoon, mould the meringue into oval cloud shapes, and poach gently for five minutes, turning once, until set.
4. Remove the meringues with a slotted spoon, drain on some kitchen paper, and put aside.

To serve

1. Swirl the custard on a plate in a wavy pattern, float the clouds on top, and encircle with the lemon curd.
2. Top with fresh strawberries, and garnish with a candied lemon peel and mint sprigs.

ICE CREAM

Amanda Stansfield, Owner/Managing Director of Granny Gothards in Stoke St Gregory, Somerset, says that ingredients and attention to detail are key to producing award-winning ice creams

Granny Gothards is an artisan ice cream maker with an extensive range including sorbets and frozen yoghurt. "We make the kind of ice cream that chefs would make," explains Amanda. "We start with the very finest ingredients – free-range egg yolks, local milk fresh from the morning's milking and, of course, the famous South West double cream – and we don't add anything artificial. Our sorbets are made with the same attention to the quality of ingredients, using only the finest fruits and purées, and, once again, nothing artificial is added. After all, nature provides the very best flavours," she continues.

With over 195 flavours on offer, a feature of Granny Gothards is its Bespoke Flavour Development Service. "This allows chefs to design an ice cream that will work on their menu, which has led to some weird and wonderful creations, for example, our Molotov Ice Cream," says Amanda. It was developed for a Portuguese restaurant and is based on the Molotov dessert, with a salted caramel ice, handmade meringues and toasted hazelnuts.

"We've had a couple of disasters when designing flavours – a pea sorbet was a definite no-no," laughs Amanda. "However, our Bloody Mary Sorbet features as part of a starter in a number of high-end restaurants."

Amanda explains that because the team has to please chefs, customers can be assured that if it becomes part of a menu or ends up in its own Granny Gothards pot, it's been approved by the best in the business!

The company is now an international brand, with regular shipments to the Middle East and China, and looking to expand into Australia, South Africa and Canada. Amanda says: "I remember being contacted by a chef in Taunton (10 miles down the road), who wanted to arrange a tasting. I asked where he heard about our ice creams and he said he was on holiday in Dubai and had them there! The world is a very small place and word gets around."

Amanda is, quite rightly, proud of her team and achievements. "We have great customers – both here and overseas – and it really is a joy to do this job. Coming into work every day, speaking to our customers and seeing the pleasure on their faces when they taste our ices is always a proud moment. Also, our team is brilliant. Working with them and feeding off their enthusiasm and creativity is amazing."

Award-winning products
2019 – Salted Caramel Ice Cream: gold; Dairy Free Chocolate Ice Cream: commended

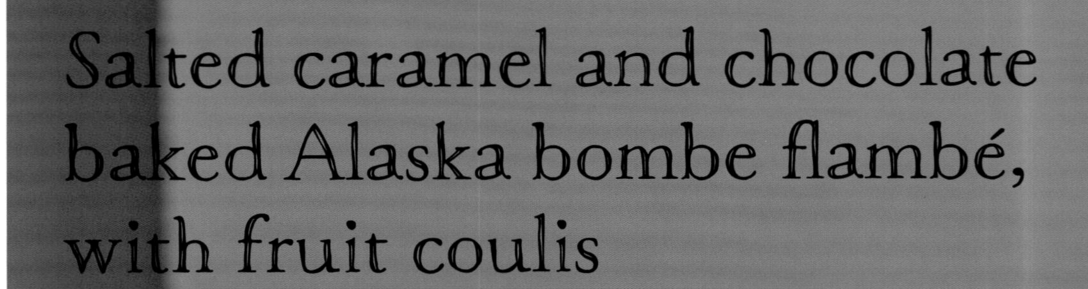

Salted caramel and chocolate baked Alaska bombe flambé, with fruit coulis

Recipe by Owen Isaacs, Executive Head Chef,
The Grand Hotel, Torquay, Devon

Ingredients

1 tub of Granny Gothards Salted Caramel Ice Cream
Dark chocolate sponge disks (homemade, or cut up a cake)
70% dark chocolate, melted
200g fruits of the forest frozen berries
50g golden caster sugar
4 spherical cake moulds

For the meringue

1 egg white
2 tbsp caster sugar
Vanilla essence

For serving

A handful of fresh raspberries
4 sprigs of mint
Brandy (to flambé)

To prepare

Preheat the oven to 200°C/180°fan/gas mark 6.

To make the coulis

Place the frozen fruit in a pan, add the sugar and simmer for 10 minutes until it's defrosted and a syrup has formed. Set aside to cool.

To make the baked Alaska bombe

1. Line a mould with clingfilm, allowing some extra film to hang over the edges.
2. Place a thin layer of chocolate sponge into the bottom of the mould.
3. Top with a scoop of ice cream, and top with another chocolate sponge disc, gently pushing the edges of the sponge around the ice cream to encase it. Freeze until set firm.

To make the meringue

1. Whisk the egg white until soft peaks are formed, then add the caster sugar (little by little) and continue whisking until stiff. Add a few drops of vanilla essence.
2. Take the bombe from the freezer and remove from the mould. Cover with the meringue and return to the freezer to set.
3. When ready to serve, remove from the freezer and place in the oven for five to ten minutes, until golden brown.

To serve

1. Place the baked Alaska bombe on the plate and swirl the coulis around it.
2. Top with fresh raspberries and garnish with a mint sprig.
3. If you wish to add the brandy, pour a little over the pudding when it's at the table and light it.

Chef's tip: It is important to keep the ice cream frozen throughout. If you're adding the brandy, warm slightly before setting it alight and don't pour too much over, or it may burn.

Chocolate ice cream with chilli and pumpkin seed granola

Ingredients
Granny Gothards Dairy Free Chocolate Ice Cream

For the granola
300g rolled jumbo oats
2 level tbsp cocoa powder
1 tbsp cinnamon
1 tsp chilli flakes
¼ tsp nutmeg
75g pumpkin seeds
100g runny honey
100g coconut oil, melted
100g freeze-dried raspberries

To make the granola

1. Preheat the oven to 180°/160° fan/gas mark 4, and line a baking tray with parchment paper.
2. In a large bowl, mix the oats, cocoa powder, cinnamon, chilli flakes, nutmeg and pumpkin seeds together.
3. In a small bowl, mix the honey and coconut oil. Add the wet ingredients to the dry and coat thoroughly.
4. Transfer the mixture to the tray and bake for 15 minutes.
5. Remove from the oven and stir with a spoon, then bake for a further 10 minutes.
6. Remove the granola from the oven and allow to cool. Break up any large chunks with your hands and stir the raspberries through. This will make more than you need but you can combine any leftovers with yoghurt for breakfast.

To serve
Sprinkle the granola in a circle on plate. Place a scoop of ice cream in the centre of the circle.

FUDGE

Dannee McGuire, Director of Roly's Fudge in Woodbury Salterton, Devon, says that finest quality ingredients are used in all of its fudge flavours, making them multi-award-winning products

Since 1987, Roly's Fudge pantries have been making homemade artisan fudge from a recipe passed down through generations. "Our fudge is a crumbly, melt-in-the-mouth variety that we make in full view of customers using ingredients that we source as naturally and close to home as we can," explains Dannee.

"We put finest quality ingredients into all of our fudge flavours," Dannee continues. "For example, our Rum 'n' Raisin doesn't use a synthetic flavouring and is full of dark rum and juicy raisins. A lot of people come in and say that it tastes just like how their grandmothers used to make it."

As it's a family-owned company, Dannee helps to run the business along with the other directors – her mum, Carrie, and brother, Matt. "Getting to celebrate big moments as a family is a good feeling," she says, reflecting on her successes with Roly's Fudge. "Winning at the Taste of the West Awards is incredible, but the little moments are just as special. I love serving a customer who's unsure about fudge, then they come back into the shop five minutes later telling me how amazing it is."

Working 24/7 with the business, Dannee makes the most of her snippets of free time when she can. "Nothing relaxes me more than scaling a wall at my local climbing centre. I also enjoy the rare moments when I can go on an all-day cliff walk down in Cornwall with my mum... sometimes we even manage not to talk about fudge!"

Award-winning products
2019 – Vanilla Clotted Cream Fudge: Gold; Butterscotch Fudge: Gold; Ginger Fudge: Gold; Raspberry & White Chocolate Fudge: Gold; Sea Salt Fudge: Gold; Salted Maple & Pecan Fudge: Gold; Coffee & Cream Fudge: Gold; Chocolate Orange Fudge: Silver; Honeycomb Fudge: Silver; Strawberry & Champagne Fudge: Silver; Vegan Chocolate Orange Fudge: Silver; Baileys Fudge: Silver

2020 – Cherry Bakewell Fudge: Gold; Double Chocolate Fudge: Gold; Peanut Butter Fudge: Gold; Vanilla Clotted Cream Fudge: Gold; Maple & Walnut Fudge: Gold; Rum 'n' Raisin Fudge: Gold; Carrot Cake Fudge: Silver

Hot vanilla clotted cream fudge soufflé

Recipe by Harrison Brockington, Head Chef, Gather, Totnes, Devon

Ingredients

For the fudge crème patissiere
280ml milk
80g Roly's Vanilla Clotted Cream Fudge
4 egg yolks
40g caster sugar
30g custard powder

For the soufflé
220g egg whites
60g caster sugar (plus extra for lining the moulds)
80g crème patisserie
20g butter, softened

Chef's tip: I like to add a spoonful of clotted cream to top it off.

To make the crème patissiere

1. Heat the milk on a medium setting in a saucepan and add the fudge to melt.
2. Meanwhile, lightly whisk the egg yolks, sugar and custard powder in a bowl.
3. Once the fudge has melted, pour half the mixture slowly over the egg mixture while whisking, to temper the eggs.
4. Pour this back into the saucepan and cook over a medium heat, whisking continuously until thickened.
5. Pour into a container, cover and refrigerate until cool.

To make the soufflé

1. Preheat the oven to 230°C/210°C fan/gas mark 8.
2. Butter four moulds, or ramekins, using a brush in upward strokes to help the soufflé rise.
3. Dust with the sugar and tap to remove any excess, then freeze.
4. Whip the egg whites into soft peaks, add the sugar, then whip to stiff peaks.
5. In a bowl, fold a quarter of the egg whites into the crème patissiere to loosen the mixture, before gently folding in the rest, taking care to keep the mix as light as possible.
6. Fill the moulds. Using a pallet knife, level the top, then run some kitchen roll around the edge to create an indentation. This helps the soufflé to rise.
7. Place the soufflés onto a tray, then into the oven for 12 minutes.
8. Remove from the oven and serve immediately.

Banana bread

Recipe by Sara Felix, Owner, Sara's Petite Cuisine, Topsham, Devon

Ingredients

3 ripe bananas (around 350g)
1 banana, for decoration
325g light brown sugar
75ml rapeseed oil
75ml alternative milk (I used oat milk)
375g self-raising flour
150g Roly's Vegan Chocolate Orange Fudge (add more if you want extra fudge!)
Pinch of salt
½ tsp of vanilla essence

Method

1. Preheat the oven to 165°C, and line a loaf tin with parchment paper.
2. Peel the three ripe bananas and place in a mixing bowl.
3. Beat the bananas, then add the sugar, oil and milk to the bowl, and mix together until well combined.
4. Add the flour, salt and vanilla to the bowl and stir until it all comes together. Don't over mix – the batter should be thick.
5. Cut the fudge into small pieces and fold into the cake batter.
6. Spoon the batter into the tin, smoothing the top with the back of a spoon.
7. Peel the extra banana, cut it in half lengthways, and place both sides on top of the batter.
8. Bake for 50 to 60 minutes, or until a skewer inserted into the middle of the cake comes out clean.

Thank you to the following Taste of the West award winners who made this recipe book possible

Beeden & Beeden
Luttrell House
Royal Oak Court
Winsford
Minehead
Somerset TA24 7JE
01643 851357

The Blackmore Vale Butchery
Unit 1a
Harding's Business Centre
Bowbridge
Henstridge
Somerset BA8 0TF
01747 838881
bmv-butchery.co.uk

The Book and Bucket Cheese Company Ltd
Manor Farm
Unit 2 Cranborne
Wimborne
Dorset BH21 5RL
01258 446177
thebookandbucket cheesecompany.co.uk

Catch of the Day
Unit 4, The Fish Quay
Sutton Harbour
Plymouth
Devon PL4 0LH
07974 473619

Cox & Laflin
Ullacombe Farm
Haytor Road
Bovey Tracey
Devon TQ13 9LL
01364 661100
coxandlaflin.co.uk

Deli Farm Charcuterie
Deli Farm
Delabole
Cornwall PL33 9BZ
01840 214106
delifarmcharcuterie.co.uk

The Eastbury Hotel & Spa, Seasons Restaurant
Long Street
Sherborne
Dorset DT9 3BY
01935 813131
theeastburyhotel.co.uk

Fordington Gin
7 South Walks Road
Dorchester
Dorset DT1 1ED
01258 454840
fordingtongin.co.uk

Fussels Fine Foods Ltd
Church Farm
Parkgate Lane
Rode
Frome
Somerset BA11 6AA
01373 831286
fusselsfinefoods.co.uk

Gather
50 Fore Street
Totnes
Devon TQ9 5RP
01803 866666
gathertotnes.com

The Grand Hotel
The Seafront
Torquay
Devon TQ2 6NT
0800 005 2244
richardsonhotels.co.uk

Granny Gothards
Unit B5
Ethmar Court
Mid Devon Business Park
Devon EX15 2EZ
01823 491591
grannygothards.co.uk

The Lordleaze Hotel
Henderson Drive
Forton Road
Chard
Somerset TA20 2HW
01460 61066
lordleazehotel.com

Moran's Restaurant & Bar
Golf Links Road
Westward Ho!
Bideford
Devon EX39 1LH
01237 472070
moransrestaurant.co

P&K Meats
Unit 8 Bayliss Centre
147 High Street
Street
Somerset BA16 0EX
01458 441439

JC & RH Palmer Ltd
West Bay Road
Bridport
Dorset DT6 4JA
01308 422396
palmersbrewery.com

Ostlers Cider Mill
Goodleigh
Barnstaple
Devon EX32 7NR
01271 321241
ostlerscidermill.co.uk

Roly's Fudge
Unit 10D
Mill Park Industrial Estate
Woodbury Salterton
Exeter
Devon EX5 1EL
01392 201059
rolysfudge.co.uk

Sara's Petite Cuisine
80 Fore Street
Topsham
Exeter
Devon EX3 0HQ
07557 474084
saraspetitecuisine.co.uk

Thatchers Cider
Myrtle Farm
Station Road
Sandford
Winscombe
Somerset BS25 5RA
01934 822862
thatcherscider.co.uk

The Three Horseshoes
Mill Street
Burton Bradstock
Dorset DT6 4QZ
01308 897259
threehorseshoes
burtonbradstock.co.uk

The Victory Inn
Victory Steps
St Mawes
Cornwall TR2 5DQ
01326 270324
victoryinn.co.uk

The Wasabi Company
Waddock Cross
Dorchester
Dorset DT2 8QY
01929 463824
thewasabicompany.co.uk

The Watercress Company
Waddock Cross
Dorchester
Dorset DT2 8QY
01929 463241
thewatercresscompany.co.uk